M000190592

The Wind ... In Our Wings

A Collection of Seasonal Meditations

Barbara J. Mosher

PublishAmerica
Baltimore

© 2005 by Barbara J. Mosher.
All rights reserved. No part of this book may be reproduced, stored in a retrieval system or transmitted in any form or by any means without the prior written permission of the publishers, except by a reviewer who may quote brief passages in a review to be printed in a newspaper, magazine or journal.

First printing

ISBN: 1-4137-7487-3
PUBLISHED BY PUBLISHAMERICA, LLLP
www.publishamerica.com
Baltimore

Printed in the United States of America

Some selections are taken from my writings
as they first appeared in:

From The Ministerium:
The Salamanca Press: 1997-1999.
Salamanca, New York

Chapel Echoes:
Valley Chapel. 1999-2001.
Warsaw Free Methodist Church,
Warsaw, New York.

The Flame:
Johnsonburg United Methodist Church,
Johnsonburg, New York.

Reprinted with permission.

Scripture taken from the Holy Bible, New International Version, NIV, Copyright 1973, 1978, 1984 by International Bible Society. Used by permission of Zondervan. All rights reserved.

Other books by Barbara Mosher:
Beyond the Yellow Brick Road

Names and identities of some of the persons and places in this book have been changed in order to protect their privacy.

This book is dedicated to the congregation of the Johnsonburg United Methodist Church, which has given me support and encouragement.

Acknowledgments

My heartfelt thanks to my husband, Ron, who steadfastly typed and computerized the manuscript, and to Susan Murphy, who edited the work and gave valuable comments. Also thanks to Danielle, Todd, and Sarah Mosher for technical help and encouragement. I couldn't have done it without you.

Most of all, if there is anything in this book that ministers to you, it is from the inspiration of the Holy Spirit, which brought many people and experiences into my life to teach me. From these I have gained greater knowledge of Him and expect that the reader will, as well. To God be the glory!

Table of Contents

SUMMER

AUTUMN

WINTER

Introduction

"He makes the clouds his chariot and rides on the wings of the wind." (Psalm 104:3)

"Then I looked up—and there before me were two women, with the wind in their wings!" (Zechariah 5:9)

"The wind blows wherever it pleases...so it is with everyone born of the Spirit." (John 3:8)

Poetically, the scriptures compare the moving of God's Holy Spirit to the moving of the wind. Jesus picks up on this thought and tells us that this is true with everyone born of the Spirit.

Wherever we travel, be it in mind, spirit, body or soul, the wind of the Holy Spirit blows us along. Buoying us up, it is indeed the wind in our wings which keeps us going and lifts us ever higher. Sometimes a gentle breeze, sometimes a gale, sometimes such a stillness as to seem nonexistent, but waiting there, nonetheless.

How often that wind blows other people and experiences into our lives. We touch, and perhaps remain a while, and then, like dry leaves, whirl away. But the impressions left on us are lasting, making marks that become part of us. It is of such people and places that I write. I share these experiences hoping they will stretch and delight and give thought to the reader, until that time when we all get to join with that One who rides on the wings of the wind.

"He stirs up His breezes
and the waters flow"
(Psalm 147:18)

Explaining Easter

While taking a Human Service course some years ago in college, I was assigned a practicum, working with recent immigrants to the U.S. from Asia and Iran. After getting to know the students by visiting them in their homes and helping them with English, the teacher gave me the job of teaching them about Easter.

To illustrate my project, I gathered up material, mostly pictures, to help bridge the language gap. In that sunny classroom of 7 or 8 students, I held up pictures of new life: flowers, bunnies, and chicks popping out of eggs. "Oh yes," they smiled, nodding their heads. They understood. Next I got out my Jesus pictures. This would be tougher. I showed them the triumphal entry—Jesus on donkey-back and people waving palm branches. They seemed to get the idea.

But the trial and crucifixion of Christ puzzled them. Why would anyone want to kill a holy man? The picture of the crucifixion repulsed them. "Ugh. Horrible." One young man from Laos decided that it was another example of American violence. "No, no," I quickly corrected. "This was long ago, in a far away country, Israel." They wondered why I was interested in this ancient event. I struggled to convey the meaning. Jesus was placed in the tomb, dead. How well they understood death. Some of them were in the U.S. because they had been driven out of their homeland by treachery.

My next picture showed an angel on top of the tomb and Jesus, the Son of God, alive, surrounded by light, and coming out of the tomb. There was polite silence while I excitedly did my best to explain the resurrection. Did they believe it? Sly eyes looked at each other with an expression that said, "You really don't expect us to believe this, do you?" Finally, a young man from Laos spoke up, trying to be helpful. "Oh yes," he nodded, "American Buddha."

I went home realizing that the resurrection of Christ really is incredible. It takes faith to appreciate it, to believe it. I had given them the "good news", but wondered like Isaiah, "Lord, who has believed our message?" (Is. 53:1). The apostle Paul responded to that question saying,

"...faith comes from hearing the message, and the message is heard through the word of Christ." (Romans. 10:17)

My hope was that I had planted a seed. Only God could make it grow and blossom into faith.

God's Messengers

When I was in sixth grade, a group of us girls used to roller skate around town. On a bright Saturday morning, off we would skate, up one street and down the next. One morning as we passed by "the millionaire's" gate, it was open. One of the bolder girls suggested that we skate into his garden. We timidly followed. It was a formal garden with a sidewalk that went around the perimeter. Feeling strange on someone's private property, we didn't venture very far. As we turned to retreat, our eyes met with a wall covered with roses. All along the side of that walled-in garden they were blooming in profusion, heavenly light pink little roses with no prickers on them. Since they spilled out in abundance, we began to pick armfuls of them.

Then immediately, like winged couriers, we flew out of the garden, giggling over our good fortune, yet fearful lest somebody see us.

Nearby was the town cemetery, located on a hill. Its red brick driveway split in either direction to encircle the knoll. Enclosed in black wrought iron spiked fencing, with well-kept green lawn, it seemed inviting. Up the hill we skated, roses in our arms, our skates bumping/clattering over the bricks. Finally we came to the back of the cemetery. The brick road led to a narrowed black-topped drive, passing by the grander tombstones, to an area with smaller, less majestic grave sites.

Our young hearts longed to do something significant with the flowers. Should we put them on a grave? That seemed like a good idea. But where? Then one of the girls spotted it, on an inconspicuous spot: a small, white-painted cross. It looked hand-made. We drew close to look at it. On the cross was written one word—BABY. "Oh, how sad. How terrible." We were touched. A baby was buried there. Of course we would put our flowers on this grave. Our heavenly pink roses circled the little grave in abundance.

Then we left. It was time to go home. We skated out of the cemetery, our skates rattling over the red bricks as we made our rapid descent.

I have thought about that incident since. Never before or after had we skated into the millionaire's garden. And we *never* picked anyone's flowers. Yet, that spring morning, in one accord, we carried out an unplanned task. At least, unplanned by us.

Perhaps the mother or father of that lost little one came to the cemetery that day after we left and, seeing the unexpected roses on the little grave, felt the breath of God's love speak to her/his grieving heart.

We never know when God might use us as his special messengers. Maybe you will be one today.

"Go, swift messengers...." (Isaiah 18:2)
"For the Lord comforts his people...." (Isaiah 49:13)

That Yields Its Fruit in Season

It was a cold March day at Lay Speakers' School, a program sponsored by the church conference to help lay people (non-clergy) learn how to express their faith. My church had paid the way for me to attend.

I listened to different people sharing their spiritual insight—Angie talked about the necessity of developing a personal theology before you could vocalize it. Steve spoke about "spiritual muggers" who accosted the unsuspecting person on the street demanding to know if he or she was saved. Charles questioned whether anger and humility could be manifested together at the same time.

Although this talk was interesting and even delightful to me, I began to feel a pang of inferiority. As the conversation progressed, nothing wise, insightful, profound, or even catchy had jumped into my mind. What did I have to share? These people all seemed to have some spiritual insight that the moment called for, and they expressed it in a few well-chosen words. I felt an awareness of my lack in comparison with them.

I went upstairs to my room and looked out the window toward the lake, covered by ice and snow. The trees by the lake reached their branches up to the sky. Something inside me said, "Don't be competitive about spiritual things, 'He is like a tree planted by streams of water that yields its fruit in its season'." The bare trees outside the window seemed to say, "It's not time for us to yield our fruit yet." They stood there patiently with arms reaching up to heaven, knowing that before long they would leaf and bud and bear fruit. Some will have blossoms, some will have seedlings; each tree will be a little different from the other and will put forth different fruit. That fruit will be produced in its season. Not before. Neither will its leaf wither.

Did you ever try to grow anything out of season? I suppose that greenhouse specialists know how to do it with their artificial environments, but my children weren't so lucky. They came home from school with what they thought was a great idea. Into tin cans filled with soil they planted green bean seeds. They carefully watered them. The bean seeds sprouted all right in their cans on the kitchen windowsill. They proceeded to grow very, very fast and very, very tall, with healthy-looking stems and leaves. We had expectations of a bean crop. But one morning to our dismay, the plants were all bent over and withered. They hadn't produced any beans. We had tried to force them to grow out of season. Rather than prosper, they died.

So it is with us, I think, if we try to force spiritual growth on our own or conjure up insight. In fact, there is no such thing as forcing spiritual growth. There may be a false appearance of spiritual growth put forth by mimicking someone else's words of wisdom or pretending to own a depth we do not have, much as the bean plants seemed to be thriving in the tin cans. But unless what we have to say comes from our experience and understanding which God has nourished, it is without real depth, and is not indeed planted by streams of living water.

Thus I think that the answer to spiritual growth is to stay close to God, that stream of living water, and wait for the season of growth which will finally take place. My time would come.

"But his delight is in the law of the Lord, and on his law he meditates day and night. He is like a tree planted by streams of water, which yields its fruit in season and whose leaf does not wither. Whatever he does prospers." (Psalm 1: 2, 3)

Good Friday

Jesus is dying
and I am sitting in church listening to traffic go by outside on the
street.

Jesus is dying
and I am home wondering what to have for supper.

Jesus is dying
and I'm coloring Easter eggs for the Easter baskets.

Jesus is dying
and I'm packing clothes to go on vacation.

Jesus is dying
and I'm thinking about personal problems.

Jesus is dying.

Jesus, did I crucify you

when I made that mean remark to my husband this morning?

Jesus, did I crucify you
when I told my little son, "Don't bother me now, I'm busy. I'll
look at your school papers later"?

Jesus, did I crucify you
when I didn't bother to visit the widow up the street?

Jesus, did I crucify you
when I rationalized why I didn't need to help a homeless person?

Jesus, did I crucify you
by being critical of my friend?

Jesus, did I crucify you
and never even know it?

Jesus is dying
And I am crying.

I'm sorry, Jesus.

Every Knee Shall Bow

We don't hear much about virtue nowadays. To obtain moral excellence doesn't seem to be a striving of the American people, young or old. While the list of virtues missing from our culture is ever growing, one in particular is absent from the American psyche. What is it? Do you have this virtue?

If you are proud of your accomplishments—you haven't got it.

If you want lots of money—you haven't got it.

If you always stand up for your rights—you haven't got it.

If you believe you deserve recognition—you haven't got it.

If you think "saving face" is important—you haven't got it.

If you like the best seat, best food, best service—you haven't got it.

If you consider yourself above the riffraff—you haven't got it.

If you have to excuse all your mistakes—you haven't got it.

What is it you haven't got? Humility.

Lest we confuse ourselves, first let me list what humility is not. It is not:

—being a doormat and letting everybody walk all over you

— having self-hatred or self-denigration

— forcing yourself into a straight jacket of good behavior
— having no backbone or fortitude
— being overconscientious or merciless with ourselves
— denying ourselves any pleasures.

Humility is freedom from pride. It is an attitude espousing humbleness, submission, and servitude to God. Does that sound undesirable; uninteresting; depressing, or boring?

Think again. Moses was considered meek and humble. Look what God was able to do through him:
— part the waters of the Red Sea
— lead two million Israelites out of bondage into freedom
— defeat the most powerful man in the known world: the pharaoh of Egypt
— present God's rules for self-government (The 10 Commandments) to his people
— see God face-to-face
— live to be 120 years old, with eyes that were not weak and strength that did not wane.

Sound boring? Uninteresting? Moses had the fullest, most exciting life you can imagine.

And where would humankind be without the humility of Jesus Christ? He *"humbled himself on a cross!"* (Philippians 2:8), and this for the remission of our sins, that we might be reconciled to God.

Palm Sunday is the beginning of Holy Week, not vacation week, not fun week, not even an ordinary week. It is a week to remember that were it not for Christ's humility, we would all be doomed to everlasting death. It is a week to bow on our knees and to confess our sins and to praise God for Christ's sacrifice. It is a week to practice humility.

"At the name of Jesus every knee should bow, in heaven and on earth and under the earth, and every tongue confess that Jesus Christ is Lord, to the glory of God the Father."
(Philippians 2:10,11)

Jesus and the Woman

Now the Passover and the Feast of Unleavened Bread were only two days away, and the chief priests and the teachers of the law were looking for some sly way to arrest Jesus and kill him.

"But not during the feast," they said, "or the people may riot."

While he was in Bethany, reclining at the table in the home of a man known as Simon the Leper, a woman came with an alabaster jar of very expensive perfume, made of pure nard. She broke the jar and poured the perfume on his head.

Some of those present were saying indignantly to one another, "Why this waste of perfume? It could have been sold for more than a year's wages and the money given to the poor." And they rebuked her harshly.

"Leave her alone," said Jesus. "Why are you bothering her? She has done a beautiful thing to me. The poor you will always have with you, and you can help them any time you want. But you will not always have me. She did what she could. She poured perfume on my body beforehand to prepare for my burial. I tell you the truth, wherever the gospel is preached throughout the world, what she has done will also be told, in memory of her."

(Mark 14: 1-9)

During the season of Lent, we think of Jesus in those last days on his way to Calvary.

The story of Jesus and Judas is one of treachery, betrayal by a friend, and the agony it must have caused Jesus. But on the way to the cross, Jesus also encountered something beautiful. One of these occasions was his encounter with the woman at the home of a man known as Simon the Leper (undoubtedly he was one who had been healed of his leprosy by Jesus).

This woman comes to Jesus in the spirit of spiritual seeking. Isn't that what all of us are drawn to sooner or later? We're seeking something beyond ourselves, something that transcends ourselves, something that is what we call "God." There is something in us that draws us to God. "Deep calls to deep." (Ps 42:7)

You are here this morning. Why? Maybe you are a young person whose parents are dragging you here, forcing you to come. That's all right. God may speak to you and change your life in spite of yourself. Maybe you're here because church is just what you do on Sunday morning. Ho—hum. That's okay. Maybe you're here because you want to please your husband or wife. It's his idea or her idea. That's okay. Something may rub off on you.

Ah, but most of you are here because you're drawn by the Spirit of God. Perhaps you've gone through those other stages but *now* you want to find something beyond yourself. And that something is God. Hooray for you! For Jesus said, "Seek and you will find." God will make himself known to you—in Jesus.

The woman at Simon's house draws near to Jesus. She seems to be known in that household, not a stranger, and undoubtedly she knows Jesus. She wants to do something for Jesus. She is drawn by an intense love. What can she do? Love always seeks to show love in some way. Her heart throbs, for Jesus is a man with a price on his head, so to speak. Jesus has told the disciples, "We are going up to Jerusalem and the Son of Man (himself) will be betrayed to the chief priests and teachers of the law. They will condemn him to death and will hand him over to the Gentiles who will mock him and spit on him and flog him and kill him. Three days later he will rise." (Mark 10: 33, 34)

The disciples don't really believe that Jesus will die. They don't truly understand. But in her spirit, this woman understands. With love welling up inside her, she runs home to fetch the alabaster jar that holds the pure nard. Nard is a precious ointment made from a rare plant in India. It was used in the East to anoint the bodies of the dead (although that may not have been her intent). Customarily, a few drops of oil were put on the head of a guest.

She grabs that jar and runs back to Simon's house. Jesus is still there reclining at the table. Without a word, she breaks the neck of the jar and starts pouring this expensive, expensive perfume on the head of Jesus. Everyone gasps. They stop eating and look at her. They think, *What are you doing, woman?*

The perfume runs down Jesus' hair, she keeps pouring, over his ears, down his shoulders and back and chest. And what is Jesus doing? He is smiling. This extravagantly generous act of love is pleasing to him. Jesus knows that horrendous things await him, but just for now, he is bathed in the perfume of her love. The sweet pungent odor covers him and fills the room and all those sitting there breathe in its sweet smell. Ah!

Her act to him is actually an "anointing", a sacred rite for consecration, usually done with oil. (The word "Christ" means "the anointed one", the "Messiah.") A high priest should have been the one to anoint Jesus, according to the religious rituals of his time. But this woman is the chosen one to be the high priest in this case. What could be more sacred than perfect love?

The woman pours the perfume all out on Jesus. Not just a few drops, not a little dab or a handful or even a cupful—the whole thing poured out—freely given. And Jesus is not only pleased, he is indeed anointed for burial.

It is a deeply spiritual and sacred moment. A sacrament.

When we decide we want more of God, and more of Jesus, we pour out our souls to him in pure love—not expecting something back, just wanting to give. It is a sacrament to him and by it we are consecrated.

"Therefore I urge you brothers, in view of God's mercy to offer yourselves a living sacrifice— this is your act of worship." (Roman 12: 1)

But some at the table do not see this. They are not looking at what is happening in a spiritual way. I Corinthians 2: 14 tells us, *"The man without the Spirit does not accept the things that come from the Spirit of God, for they are foolishness to him, and he cannot understand them, because they are spiritually discerned."* All that these men see is a foolish woman making a big show, pouring out that expensive perfume all over Jesus—wasting it. If she had some attachment to the group, she didn't ask "their" permission. Judas was the treasurer of the group and he was especially indignant about it. He rebuked her harshly. "Why this waste of perfume? It could have been sold for more that a year's wages, and the money given to the poor."(Remember that Jesus is always concerned about the poor).

If no one had come to her rescue, the woman might have gone home weeping. But Jesus jumps to her defense. "Leave her alone", he says, "Why are you bothering her? She has done a beautiful thing to me. She did what she could. She poured perfume on my body beforehand to prepare for my burial." Then he gives *her* the great gift of telling that what she has done is so honored that it will be told in *memory of her* throughout the world—wherever the gospel (good news of Jesus) is preached." Wow!

In response to their remark that the perfume should have been sold and the money given to the poor, Jesus replied, "The poor you will always have with you, and you can help them any time you want. But you will not always have me." Was he disregarding the poor? No, of course not. Rather, he would soon be gone. It was appropriate to show him love. He was not letting them put religion in a little box. A little box that said ,"Do this. Do that" *always.*

As human beings we like to be comfortable with things, and so we put people and things in little boxes. Then we put a lid on and say, "Don't get out and disturb me." We want some things to be as they always were.

We don't want our husband, or our wife, or sometimes even our children to behave differently.

"Woman! Stay in your box. Don't do anything emotional or extravagant!"

"Religion! Stay in your box. Do the prescribed things. Don't get too personal or emotional."

"Disciples! Stay in your box. Follow cautiously, and with an eye kept to the rules!"

But Jesus opens the box, and lets the woman out, "You have done a beautiful thing for me."

Jesus opens the box and lets religion out. An act of great love supercedes the general course of action.

Jesus opens the box of discipleship and says in effect, "Look beyond the narrow confines of organized religion to what I'm doing in the world."

And Jesus opens the box for us. "Get out and be free and look around for ways to show your love." When we come to Jesus "seeking", he lets us out of our box, and into his realm. And in this freedom beautiful things happen.

The March Wind Doth Blow

There's a nursery rhyme that goes:
"The March wind doth blow
and we shall have snow
What will the robin do then, poor thing?
He'll sit himself down to keep himself warm
And hide his head under his wing, poor thing."

The month of March usually gets to me. I get irritated and annoyed more easily. If I ever get "down," it's going to be in the month of March. Discontent can set in. This happens to other people too, I notice. People decide to move south, or change jobs, or leave the church in late February or early March. There is too much winter (even when the winter is mild), too little sunshine, and too much sickness (ours or the kids). Our body elements get depleted, or we're just plain tired of looking at a barren landscape for so long.

In the Bible, Solomon is thought to have written the book of Ecclesiastes. In this book, he tries everything and searches everywhere under the sun to find meaning, only to conclude that all of our activity in life is meaningless. Nothing seems worthwhile.

34

What a pessimistic attitude. He must have written it in a dreary time of year, like our March. If he had waited until springtime, life might have looked a little better: spring rains, spring flowers, balmy breezes, and hope anew.

For the Christian, Jesus Christ and his resurrection make all the difference. He ushered in new life for all of us, both now during our lifetime here on earth, and throughout all eternity. For that reason life is not meaningless. It can never be meaningless, despite emotional ups and downs, situational advances or setbacks, and tiresome winters. Some troubles may have to be endured, but in the end there is hope. Spring does follow winter. With it comes Easter, and God's glorious gift once more.

The March wind may yet blow again with snow. And, like the robin, I will hide my head under my wing and wait it out, knowing that spring will return.

"See! The winter is past; the rains are over and gone. Flowers appear on the earth; the season of singing has come...." (Song of Songs 2:11,12)

Peter Sifted

"Simon, Simon, Satan has asked to sift you, as wheat. But I have prayed for you, Simon, that your faith may not fail. And when you have turned back, strengthen your brothers." (Luke 22: 31—32)

Then Jesus told them, "This very night you will all fall away on account of me, for it is written:

" 'I will strike the shepherd, and the sheep of the flock will be scattered.'

But after I have risen, I will go ahead of you into Galilee," Peter replied, "Even if all fall away on account of you, I never will."

"I tell you the truth," Jesus answered, "this very night, before the rooster crows, you will disown me three times."

But Peter declared, 'Even if I have to die with you, I will never disown you.' And all the other disciples said the same." (Matthew 26: 31—35).

Now Peter was sitting out in the courtyard, and a servant girl came to him. "You also were with Jesus of Galilee," she said.

But he denied it before them all. "I don't know what you're talking about," he said.

Then he went out to the gateway, where another girl saw him and said to the people there, "This fellow was with Jesus of Nazareth."
He denied it again, with an oath: "I don't know the man!"
After a little while, those standing there went up to Peter and said, "Surely you are one of them, for your accent gives you away."
Then he began to call down curses on himself and he swore to them, "I don't know the man!"
Immediately a rooster crowed. Then Peter remembered the word Jesus had spoken: "Before the rooster crows, you will disown me three times." And he went outside and wept bitterly." (Matthew 26: 69-75)

Peter was a big fisherman, a strong, hard-working man. He was a man able to withstand the storms at sea. Peter was the man who took a risk and stepped out of the boat to walk on the water during a storm, when Jesus beckoned to him.

When Peter, James, and John saw the glorification of Jesus on the mountaintop, it was Peter who was ready to put up some shelters so they could stay there.

Peter was a man of integrity, the loyal one, the steadfast one. He would never, never cave in. He would fight if necessary. He would go with Jesus even to the death.

What happened to Peter? We see him now, weeping bitterly because he publicly denied knowing Christ. He let Jesus down. Right within Jesus' hearing distance he swore that he didn't know him. In Jesus' hour of need, Peter wasn't there for him.

In Luke's gospel account we read that earlier Jesus had warned Peter. Calling him by his given name, Jesus had said, "Simon, Simon, Satan has asked to sift you as wheat." In other words, "You're going to be run through the sifter, Peter. You're going to be shaken up and bounced around. You're going to go through an ordeal. To sift as wheat means to separate the grain from the chaff. You're going to find out what's in you, Peter!

In what we refer to as the Lord's prayer, Jesus tells us to pray to God, "Lead us not into temptation, but deliver us from the evil one."

I don't want to be sifted by temptation, do you? It's a terrible experience.

Jesus doesn't say to Peter (and he doesn't say to us), "I won't let this happen to you." Instead, Jesus says, "But I have prayed for you that your faith may not fail. And when you have turned back, strengthen your brothers." That tells Peter that indeed, he will fall away for a time. Jesus even tells him the form it will take: "Peter, this very night you will disown me three times before the cock crows." What could be clearer? But Peter doesn't recognize his weakness.

The reason that God allowed Peter and allows Christians to be sifted by Satan is that we need to know where our weaknesses are. We'll know first-hand the temptations to which we are susceptible. If God is ever going to use us to further his kingdom on this earth, we need to know what our weaknesses are. They may be different than what we think they are. Only by the grace of God will we be overcomers and usable to him, and that not by our own merit.

The sifting is done to refine us. In this process, we see what we're made of. We may find that our weakness is in the area of money (greed), or illicit sex, egotistical flattery, or caring about public opinion (pride), or self-interest or "whatever." In the case of Peter, it was an inflated idea of his own integrity, "I will never fall away."

Let's not be so sure of our own righteousness, our own integrity. God is a master at providing the very situation that will prove us lacking.

Let's see how the sifting of Peter happens. Peter gets caught off-guard. Remember, it's a crisis situation. It is night on the Mount of Olives and Jesus is being arrested by the palace guards. Peter is ready to prevent that arrest. He even draws his sword and cuts off the ear of the high priest's servant. But Jesus immediately commands him, "Put your sword away!"

Okay, it is not going to be *that kind* of fight. The situation is not unfolding as Peter imagined it might. Peter is feeling out of his element. He trails along as Jesus is seized and bound and taken to the high priest.

In the courtyard of the high priest the officials and the servants are standing around warming themselves by the fire. Peter feels out of place and fearful. He is caught off-guard when a girl questions him—not a soldier, not an inquisition, not a situation where his bravery will stand out, but a servant girl who challenges him, "Surely you are not another of this man's disciples? Peter takes the easy way out. Protecting himself, he answers, " I am not."

The same thing happens again and again. The people are questioning him with strong suspicions. In answer, Peter even calls down curses upon himself to hide his identity. He feels like one of his fish, caught in a net.

Now is the time to be counted. Now is the time to say, "Yes, I follow this man. I follow Jesus." But Peter fails miserably.

At that instant, the cock crows. For a second Peter looks up, and his eyes and Jesus' meet. The truth hurts. Peter has it in himself to be a coward (just like all of us). He has it in himself to opt for his own skin in a crisis (just like all of us). He has it in him to lie (just like all of us). Peter has been sifted.

Sometimes God sifts us. Sometimes God sifts his churches, so that true believers may be separated from false. A return to true worship will result from it. Is God sifting the Episcopal Church at this time? Sometimes God sifts the nations. Is our nation being sifted in the recent Iraqi war and following crisis?

Sifting is always done to show us the truth, and to bring us to remorse, followed by our repentance.

After Peter is sifted, he goes outside and weeps bitterly. His pride is slashed to bits. He is a humbled man, awaiting the verdict.

Will Jesus hate him for being a coward? Will Jesus disown him for his lack of loyalty at a time when it was needed so badly? Will Jesus forever see Peter as a weak and unreliable man, and set him aside?

We are no different or better than Peter. We sin. We cause God grief. We are sorrowful when we see our sin. We repent. Perhaps we go out in the alley and weep.

But Jesus does not leave Peter. Nor does he leave us. It is no small thing that at the resurrection the very first words carried a message for Peter that Christ was going ahead and would see him in Galilee. At that joyful meeting Peter is reinstated by Jesus! "Feed my sheep."

Are you being sifted? Keep the faith. Have hope. It's a learning process, a strengthening process. God isn't done with you yet.

Jesus and Judas

Now the Passover and the feast of Unleavened Bread were only two days away, and the chief priests and the teachers of the law were looking for some sly way to arrest Jesus and kill him.

"But not during the Feast," they said, "or the people may riot..."

Then Judas Iscariot, one of the twelve, went to the chief priests to betray Jesus to them. They were delighted to hear this and promised to give him money. So he watched for an opportunity to hand him over.

The disciples ...went into the city and found things just as Jesus had told them. So they prepared the Passover.

When evening came, Jesus arrived with the Twelve. While they were reclining at the table eating, he said, "I tell you the truth, one of you will betray me—one who is eating with me."

They were saddened, and one by one they said to him, "Surely, not I?"

"It is one of the Twelve," he replied, "one who dips bread into the bowl with me. The Son of man will go just as it is written about him. But woe to that man who betrays the Son of man! It would be better for him if he had not been born." (Mark 14)

Then, dipping the piece of bread, Jesus gave it to Judas Iscariot, son of Simon. As soon as Judas took the bread, Satan entered into him .... As soon as Judas had taken the bread, he went out. And it was night.

(John 13)

Some time ago there was a shooting at a San Diego high school. A student went into the school and terrorized the teachers and the students by shooting into the rooms. He wounded one student. Others were hurt by flying glass as he shot out some windows. A police officer on the scene shot it out with the student, wounding him.

After this terrifying attack was over, a hue and cry went up on the TV news stations, the radio and the newspapers. Quickly, the news magazines picked it up, as well as the people on the street. "Why?" was the cry. "Why would this boy do this?" "What was the motive?" "What influenced him or drove him to it?"

As human beings, we want to know what went wrong. This act wasn't normal behavior. We want to figure out why this would happen. What went wrong?

The same question plagues us with Judas Iscariot. "What was his motive? Why did he betray Jesus, even to his death?" Judas knew what he was doing. He made contact with men of murderous intent. Judas well knew what he was doing.

The chief priests and scribes (leaders) of the Jewish religion were looking for some way to secretly arrest Jesus and kill him secretly, because they were afraid of the people. Jesus had many followers and was well-loved by the common people. In order to arrest Jesus secretly, the rulers needed someone like Judas who knew the habits of Jesus. Judas was a trusted friend who knew where Jesus went at night and where Jesus camped out in the hills. So, when Judas showed up on their doorstep, the chief priests knew he was just the man they needed. What luck! Judas was one of the Twelve, one of the inner circle. They agreed to pay him well—30 pieces of silver—if he would lead them to Jesus some night and point him out. Judas watched for an opportune time, which came up soon.

This was such a horrendous act of betrayal of a good friend, that the compulsive question of "WHY?" keeps getting asked. Somehow the story is incomplete without Judas' motive. Walter Wangerin, Jr., in his book, *Reliving The Passion*, pursues this question, and I put forth some of his thoughts on why Judas did it.

Some say it was greed. Judas got paid 30 pieces of silver—enough to buy a field. Did he do it for money? Some say that Judas was angry over the use of the group's money. He was the treasurer and had charge of the purse. Jesus had just praised the woman who poured an extremely expensive jar of perfume over him, anointing him. Judas had been indignant over that. Was it out of anger? Others say that it was misguided zealotry. Judas wanted to force Jesus to establish an "earthly" kingship. So, there is speculation.

The Gospel writers ignore these questions, and that is a lesson for us. Motives are beside the point. Motives are merely incidental. Then we have to ask ourselves, "Do our motives, rationale, or reasons make it any less of a sin?" Do we ever betray the sovereignty of the Lord Jesus in our lives? If so, isn't that always a sin, regardless of the factors that lead to it, or regardless of what factors we think forced us to it? And, aren't we very eager to defend ourselves, and "take away" from our fault by citing reasons "why" we had to do it that way? We try to justify ourselves by some situation that preceded the sin. Somehow, motives console us. That's why we want so badly to have logical motives.

Listen to our rationalizing:

It's not my fault. He hit me first. I was only protecting myself.

Don't blame me! I grew up in a bad home. My parents abused me. Blame them.

Hey man, it's a dog-eat-dog world out there. I'm only trying to survive.

I can't help the way I am. That's the way God made me. God gave me my appetites, to fill my needs.

None of this stuff justifies us. It isn't some motive before the sin that justifies us, but rather, the forgiveness of Christ, which meets our sorrow over it and repentance *after* the sin. If I did it, I'm responsible, whatever the reasons might be. If, by my excuses, I duck the responsibility as many people do, I'll never truly repent, and then the forgiveness of Christ will seem beside the point and that sin will remain on my soul. Oh, what I will have missed! But if I own up to my responsibility —own up to the sin, call it a sin—and so repent, then *that* forgiveness will justify before God even the most horrendous betrayer of Jesus. Even Judas Iscariot. Even me. The redeeming love of Jesus, could alone write a happy ending. So let's forget about looking for motives.

Let's back up and look at Jesus and Judas at the table—celebrating the Passover meal, before the horrendous act of betrayal has happened. Judas has agreed to betray Jesus to the Chief Priests. He's going to lead the palace guards to the campsite and point out Jesus to them. But Judas hasn't done it yet. He's got the blood money, but he hasn't committed the sin yet. He's still sitting at the table.

Judas has no better friend than Jesus. Nobody could love Judas more.

Out of love, not out of dislike or loathing, Jesus grants Judas a moment of terrible self-awareness. He says, "One of you will betray me, the one who is dipping bread into the dish with me." Only Judas knows who Jesus is talking about. Judas hasn't done the deed yet, but Jesus sees it coming—and while Judas yet contemplates the sin, Jesus gives him three crucial gifts. These gifts he gives to us also.

1. The gift of knowing. In speaking at the table Jesus uses the word betrayal ("One of you will betray me"). Betrayal is a strong word. No question what it means—a traitor. He lets Judas see exactly what he's about to do. Judas can't fool himself. Jesus does the same for us.

2. The gift of free will. Jesus could have stopped Judas—but he gave him free choice. The knowledge freed Judas from ignorance or any unconscious compulsion. Now he can choose whether to do the deed or not do it.

3. The gift of sole responsibility. If Judas proceeds with it, then he alone shall have done the deed.

What more can a friend do than Jesus has done? And all of this as friends intimately sharing the Passover meal. Jesus shall surely "go as it was written of him," but Judas still has the choice.

Judas could choose not to be the one to betray Jesus. He could choose the sorrowful "Yes it is I"—and confess himself a sinner—and repent and STOP! There is still time to stop, before it's too late and the deed is done.

What about us? For example, what about the married man who has such a wonderful relationship with his secretary? He's thinking about her more and more. Now he has a chance to drive her to a meeting they have to attend far away. They'll be alone together. STOP!

Or what about the student who's alone in the classroom with a teacher when the teacher gets a coughing attack and leaves the room to go to the nurse's office. The test questions are in a folder on his desk. It would be helpful to know what those questions are. STOP!

How about the bank teller who realizes that a mistake has been made in the money intake which can never be tracked or accounted for. Her bills have been piling up and she sees no way out. If she takes the money, it will be a great help to her and no one will be the wiser. STOP!

There is always time to stop. Even at the last minute. Judas has set into motion the coming events, but he *does not* turn back. He allowed Satan to enter in and guide him. The end is destruction. All seems lost. The crucifixion of Jesus takes place. Love is annihilated. Judas kills himself. The scripture says of him "Better for him if he had not been born." (Matt 26: 24) For Judas, and for those who reject Jesus, this is the end.

But the story doesn't end there for Jesus or for us—thank God. God takes that terrible crucifixion and turns it into his saving grace for our souls. The worst thing in the world has been turned into the best.

The story comes to a joyful conclusion in the life-giving resurrection.

Notes:
With thanks to Walter Wangerin Jr. for his book, *Reliving The Passion* (Grand Rapids: Zondervan Publishing House, 1992).

No Absolutes?

When our oldest son turned 18 and went off to college, he began to challenge all the values he had been taught. He would come home and engage us in discussions about right and wrong, about the Bible, about marriage, family, and politics. Everything was under fire.

Actually, I felt good about it, because deep down I knew that the unchallenged life, the unexamined life is not a worthwhile life. We all have to come to terms with who we are and what we really believe.

But Mark wanted to throw everything out. No absolute truths, no moral authority, only opinion counted. He was convinced that,"As long as I'm not hurting anybody else what does it matter?" One discussion ended with me picking up the Bible and asking, "Mark, are your opinions more trustworthy than those in this book?"

Is the Bible the authority, or not? This question is the pivotal point in our whole belief system. If there is no God, who has revealed Himself in the Bible, then we are awash in a sea of uncertainty. If the precepts set down there are not to teach us what the "good life" is, then life is in chaos. Nothing is unequivocally true or valuable. Life is indeed a "walking shadow" (Shakespeare) and we may as well give up and join the Nihilists. It ends in gloom and doom.

Total freedom from moral values and social mores does not bring about the full, joyous life, as is advertised. The "morning after" is filled with regrets and woes. One becomes worse instead of better. Enter anger, contempt, hatred, obsessive lust, divorce, verbal manipulation, revenge, slapping, suing, cursing, coercing and begging. It is the stuff of soap operas and the daily news, and real life.

What is the answer? You know it. *"Seek ye first the Kingdom of God and His righteousness, and all these things (material needs) will be added to you as well." (Jesus Christ: Matt: 6:33)*

Absolutes are set by a Being higher than ourselves; the One who created us, for our own good. They make sense out of life. They create order in our chaotic world. They are the undergirding of our purpose in life.

Read the Bible and practice what it says. It's still the word of God. It's still the Absolute.

Jesus and Pilate

When Jesus was accused by the chief priest and the elders, he gave no answer. Then Pilate asked him, "Don't you hear the testimony they are bringing against you?" But Jesus made no reply, not even to a single charge—to the great amazement of the governor.

Now it was the governor's custom at the feast to release a prisoner chosen by the crowd. At that time they had a notorious prisoner, called Barabbas. So when the crowd had gathered, Pilate asked them, "Which one do you want me to release to you? Barabbas or Jesus, who is called Christ?" For he knew it was out of envy that they had handed Jesus over to him...

But the Chief priests and the elders persuaded the crowd to ask for Barabbas and to have Jesus executed.

Which of the two do you want me to release to you?" asked the governor.

"Barabbas," they answered.

What shall I do, then, with Jesus who is called Christ?" Pilate asked.

They all answered, "Crucify him!"

"Why? What crime has he committed?" asked Pilate.

But they shouted all the louder, "Crucify him!"

When Pilate saw that he was getting nowhere, but that instead an uproar was starting, he took water and washed his hands in front of the crowd. "I am innocent of this man's blood," he said. "It is your responsibility!"

All the people answered, "Let his blood be on us and on our children!"

Then he released Barabbas to them. But he had Jesus flogged, and handed him over to be crucified.

(Matthew 27)

Was it necessary for Jesus to go before the Roman governor, Pontius Pilate?

After all, it is the Jewish leaders that have arrested him and questioned him and decided that he is guilty of blasphemy (claiming deity).

Isn't that enough? No, because at that time the Jewish government is under the power of Rome. Only the Roman governor could impose the death penalty. Since the Jewish government (the Sanhedrin) wants Jesus killed they have to convince Pilate that Jesus deserves death. The Jews do what is expedient. They believe, "It is better that one man die for the people than that the whole nation perish." (John 11:50)

Enter politics.

Early in the morning on the day we now designate as Good Friday, they take Jesus to the palace to get an audience with the governor. Perhaps Pilate is eating his breakfast in the palace, or perhaps he hasn't eaten yet.

He is summoned to go out in the courtyard to meet with the Jewish leaders. They can't come inside because their religious law forbids it. They want to be religiously correct so that they can eat the Passover. (Isn't that a powerful contradiction?)

We can image Pilate's irritation, "Those despicable Jews—and their impossible religion! Now what do they want?"

But Pilate is a professional, a politician—and he proceeds as one. Perhaps thinking, "Let's get this over with," he says with authority, "What charges are you bringing against this man?" Pilate is in charge, in control.

The Jewish leaders don't give him a straight answer—politicians seldom do. They reply, "If he were not a criminal, we would not have handed him over to you."

Pilate responds, "Take him yourself and judge him by your own law." [The last thing Pilate wants to do is get bogged down in their governmental religious disputes.] [He doesn't know anything about their religion and he doesn't care to know.]

"So far, so good," Pilate was thinking. "I'm still in charge. This incident will soon come to an end and I can get on with more important matters."

But suddenly the real reason for this early morning confrontation comes to light. The Jewish leaders want to execute this guy.

"But we have no right to execute anyone," the Jewish leaders point out. "That is the ruler's duty; the governor's duty."

Luke's gospel tells us that the Jewish leaders charge Jesus with treason, saying to Pilate, "We have found this man subverting our nation. He opposes payment of taxes to Caesar and claims to be Christ, a King."

The Jews have to contrive some charge that would be a serious transgression to the Roman law.

Notice how the charge changed. First, the Jewish leaders charged Jesus with "blasphemy." Blasphemy doesn't mean a thing to those who don't honor God. But these Jews need Pilate's decree, so they change the charge to treason. "He wants to make himself king of the Jews."

Politics play a similar role today. Take for example the war with Iraq. At first our objective was to stop the terrorists, to find and destroy weapons of mass destruction. Then, the focus became Iraqi Freedom. Politics.

This charge of Jesus wanting to be a king was serious. Pilate has to pay attention. The Jewish leaders are suddenly in charge. Pilate is the public servant, bound to his law. What is Pilate's duty in this case?

Pilate speaks to Jesus. "Are you the king of the Jews?"

"Yes. It is as you say," Jesus answers.

Now the Jewish chief priests heaped on the accusations, piling charge upon charge. Wasn't the accusation of treason enough? Come on, why are you adding all these lesser charges? It was phony.

Pilate begins to suspect some falsity here. Jesus is not answering these accusations. Finally Jesus is in control.

Pilate is rattled because Jesus isn't defending himself against these obviously trumped-up accusations. (Did you ever notice that the person who remains quiet in a hassle usually gains the most respect?)

John's gospel tells us that Pilate uses sarcasm on Jesus; this minority Jew. A put down.

Jesus doesn't react. Jesus is still in control.

Pilate is arrogant. Jesus always has been in control. They beat him. They strip him of his dignity and torment him. But, they cannot take away from him his decision on how he is going to respond. Jesus keeps his cool.

The Jewish leaders have lost theirs—screaming and yelling and accusing.

Pilate becomes uneasy and uncertain about what to do. Basically he sees Jesus as a religious man, a philosopher, a deep thinker, plus Jesus is obviously stirring up the Jewish leaders, but is no threat to the Roman Empire—no rebel, like Barabbas. Jesus tells Pilate that his kingdom is not of this earth.

An idea strikes Pilate—the custom of releasing a prisoner during the Jewish Passover. Since Pilate sees Jesus as innocent, he hopes that perhaps the Jewish crowd will press to have Jesus released and he will be done with it.

It is a good idea, but the Jewish leaders have too much at stake and too much influence. They want Jesus out of their hair and executed. So they stir up the volatile crowd to ask for Barabbas. "Release Barabbas!"

John's gospel tells us that Pilate then had Jesus flogged. Blood running down his face, Jesus staggering, a crown of thorns on his head, he is again brought out before the people. Pilate hopes that when they see this man Jesus in such an obviously pitiful condition, their hearts will soften. Their lust for bloodshed will be satisfied.

"Once more, Pilate came out and said to the Jews, 'Look, I am bringing him out to you to let you know that I find no basis for a charge against him.'"

Pilate presents Jesus to them, "Here is the man." But it doesn't work. Their hearts remain hardened. As soon as the chief priests and officials see Jesus, they shout, "Crucify, crucify!"

The crowd is apparently in control. A mob can riot and take over in an instant. A crowd is a power to be feared. (If you've ever seen a crowd out of control, bent on destruction, you know what I mean). To prevent a riot Pilate releases Barabbas. He delivers Jesus up to be crucified. Jesus will die.

Pilate does what is expedient. (It is better that one innocent man die than that I have a riot on my hands and lose control of the mob and of my position). It is at this time, in front of the people, that Pilate takes water and washes his hands saying, "I am innocent of this man's blood. The responsibility is yours."

In this scenario, Pilate seems to be a terrible man, inhuman, weak, acting out of personal interest and political necessity. But now that I have experienced being the person in charge of an organization I can see how he may have felt caught in the middle.

Consider how you might respond in the following situations:

Suppose an elderly mother or father needs to be put in a nursing home. The family gathers. One irate member says, "You go ahead and do what you are going to do, but I wash my hands of it. I will not take the responsibility!"

A city puts out a decree, "No religious symbols will be displayed in this city at any time—not at any holiday or on any court-house wall." The Christians are hurt but do not seek to change the law, in effect saying, "We wash our hands of it."

Germany and France said of the Iraqi war, "Not our responsibility. We wash our hands of it."

Pilate washes his hands, but the responsibility never leaves him. Jesus' face would forever be before him. History tells us that in the course of time Pilate was deposed from power, degraded, and driven into exile, where he committed suicide.

And who was in control all the time? Jesus was, all the while.

In his examination by Pilate, Jesus tells him, "You would have no power over me if it were not given from above." (John 19: 11)

And prior to that in the garden of Gethsemane when he was arrested, Jesus said to his disciples, "Do you think I cannot call on my Father, and he will at once put at my disposal twelve legions of angels? But how then would the Scriptures be fulfilled that say it must happen in this way?" Jesus went as it was decreed.

Ultimately, God's will was done. It was better that Jesus die than that we perish in our sins.

So we see:

Jesus was in control all the time. He let the course of events happen. He gave up his life that in the end, we might be set free from sin and death. Pilate was one player in the drama. God knew that Pilate would, when caught in a tight spot, opt for what was expedient, rather than what was right. The course of events was allowed to happen.

But woe to the man through which they happened.

Notes:

With thanks to Walter Wangerin, Jr. for his book, *Reliving The Passion* (Grand Rapids: Zondervan Publishing House, 1992).

On Prayer

If you did not grow up in a praying family, perhaps your first experience in prayer was during a crisis time in your life. You looked up into the sky and cried out, "God, if you're really real, I need help!" Then you begged God to intercede and act on your behalf. If things turned out the way you wanted, you may have thanked God and decided that he was there and that he was on your side. He had looked upon you with favor in your time of need. You would pray again when the occasion arose. If things turned out badly for you, after your prayer for help, you may have concluded that if there was a God, he didn't answer prayer, or at least not your prayer. You doubted your ability to reach God.

The question is, "How does prayer work? When prayer is our heart's desire to make contact with our Creator, we are ready to learn, for prayer is a learned skill. If you wanted to learn how to swim, the best time would not be when your boat is sinking in the ocean, although you would certainly be jolted into realizing your necessity at that time. Likewise, learning to pray and hear God's answer is best done in a time of quiet concentration. A crisis in life may have made you realize your dire need of God, but in your groping emergency, you didn't know how to make contact. But you tried. That is worth a great deal, for it shows that you do know the answer is prayer.

Now take time to learn to pray. It's not so bad. When you tried to learn how to swim you got water up your nose. You splashed and splashed and sunk to the bottom. You wanted to give up but you kept at it. Your friends cheered you on. Before long you were gliding in the water and it was immensely enjoyable. Prayer can be like that. Contact with the Almighty! Answers. Guidance. Love that flows. Strength in understanding. Vision. Inspiration. Endurance. God wants to make contact with His creatures. The avenue is prayer. Try it. Work at it. Learn it. You will be blessed.

God's Unfailing Love
by Kristine Mosher Butts

It was a beautiful spring day—one that promoted the feeling of love and rebirth. But I was feeling anything but love.

A few months earlier, my husband of fourteen years had left me and our two sons. Now, looking out my window at the newfound spring, I was full of anger and self-pity. How dare spring arrive in all its splendor when I had no one to share it with, no one to love! I felt so alone. It just wasn't fair.

In anguish I cried, "Lord, I need love. Please, Lord, send me love!"

A couple of days later, as I was looking over my children's school papers, I noticed, much to my surprise, that my ten-year-old son, Zenon, had written across the top of his math paper, "I love you, Mom." Strange, I thought, he had never done that before. For the next five days, all the school papers Zenon brought home were the same. Across the top of each of them he had written "I love you, Mom," and with some he had even drawn rainbows.

The messages were not limited only to school work. On my bedroom dresser I found a tiny piece of paper and on it the tiny words: "I love you, Mom." Larger messages appeared in the kitchen, on the floor in the den, on paper bags, and even on the front seat of the car! During the entire week it seemed that everything I touched or turned over had written on it: "I love you, Mom." But not once did Zenon ever mention anything about these "messages."

Then, as suddenly as the messages started, they stopped. And then I knew. Jesus had answered my desperate prayer and had brought me love through my son. I knew something else then, too. Jesus loved me, and I would never be alone.

Let your face shine on your servant; save me in your unfailing love." (Psalm 31: 16)

Mother as Servant

Then the mother of Zebedee's sons came to Jesus with her sons and, kneeling down, asked a favor of him,

"What is it you want?" he asked.

She said, "Grant that one of these two sons of mine may sit at your right and the other at your left in your kingdom."

"You don't know what you are asking," Jesus said to them. "Can you drink the cup I am going to drink?"

"We can," they answered.

Jesus said to them, "You will indeed drink from my cup, but to sit at my right or left is not for me to grant. These places belong to those for whom they have been prepared by my Father."

When the ten heard about this, they were indignant with the two brothers. Jesus called them together and said, "You know that the rulers of the Gentiles lord it over them, and their high officials exercise authority over them. Not so with you. Instead, whoever wants to become great among you must be your servant, and whoever wants to be first must be your slave—just as the Son of Man did not come to be served, but to serve, and to give his life as a ransom for many."

(Matt. 20: 20-28)

If you are a woman and read the title of this sermon, "Mother As Servant," you may have had a strong reaction.

You may have thought, "Mother as a servant—boy, that's what I am! I work and not only that, I have to cook and clean and shop and keep track of all the household expenses and do all the dirty jobs as well as take care of the kids! And I'm sick and tired of it! So don't glorify mother as a servant or I'm going to puke and get up and walk out of here. My family may honor me on Mother's Day, but the rest of the year it's: "Mom, why don't I have any clean T-shirts? Mom, I have to have this costume ready by 4 o'clock this afternoon. Mom, I know you made supper, but I haven't got time to eat it; I have to leave now."

Mom can feel like another appliance or, if you've got little kids, it's: "Mommy, Mommy, Mommy" all day and sometimes all night. It's dirty diapers, runny noses, sticky finger marks, and endless cleaning up of messes. A stay-at-home mom's existence is one of constant demands. No wonder so many women seek to escape this role.

Yet Jesus takes that role of servanthood; serving other people in the lowliest tasks, and turns it around and exalts it to the highest place. We forget that, don't we? Instead we buy into what the world thinks of menial, servant-type jobs.

But in John 13 we read about Jesus acting as servant, the lowliest servant, by putting a towel around his waist and washing his disciples' feet. In that era and region, they wore sandals. Their feet would have been pretty cruddy, caked with dust, dirt, and dung…and stinky. The job was probably equivalent to cleaning the toilet or cleaning up after someone's vomit.

In fact, Peter is aghast at Jesus doing this foot washing. "No way!" says Peter. "You shall never wash my feet." But Jesus insists and tells him that later he will have understanding of this. The understanding is that Jesus came to serve. Even though he's their teacher and master, his desire is *to serve,* in even the lowliest task, and he tells the disciples to do likewise. "Just as the son of man did not come to be served but to serve."

By serving in this manner, Jesus took away the stigma of lowly tasks for ever and ever. No job is too lowly. The only job too lowly for Christians would be one that is immoral or illegal. So Moms, we need to re-look at our position as servant. Are we "willing servants" to other people? Joyful servants? Our attitude is all important. Do we serve in love? Do we connect our serving with that of Jesus? Do we need an attitude adjustment?

I remember some years ago I was making the bridesmaids' dresses for our daughter Gloria's wedding. Four aqua satin dresses with little ruffles all down the back. I was a pastor at the time, so every spare minute I had I spent at the sewing machine. I thought the dresses were beautiful—but I heard a lot of complaints. "This dress makes me look fat. I look terrible."

"Too tight, too loose."

"They're pretty dresses but not my style."

I began to get a bad attitude about this. Here I was, slaving away to save them money. They had picked out the pattern and material. "Grrr." There became a pout in my spirit.

Then the Lord gave me this verse: "Serve wholeheartedly, as if you were serving the Lord, not men (in this case women) because you know that the Lord will reward everyone for whatever good he does." (Ephesians 6: 7,8)

I began to talk to Jesus as I sewed. "I'm making this dress for you, Jesus. I hope you like it. I'm working for you." My attitude changed. My spirit lifted.

Our daughter, Gloria, who was the bride, did appreciate my work.

Mother as willing servant. It's a position that calls for sacrifice—of time and energy and plans. Moms know this. Maybe we'd rather go to the party, but we've got to stay home with a sick baby. Maybe we'd rather not spend an afternoon in a hot gymnasium listening to an out-of-tune Junior Band. Maybe we'd rather not spend evenings listening to a struggling reader bore us to tears. This calls for sacrifice, a willing servant—out of love.

But Mom, when you sacrifice, you've chosen the higher thing. Jesus said of those serving children, "If anyone gives a cup of cold water to one of these little ones because he is my disciple, I tell you the truth, he will certainly not lose his reward." (Matthew 10:42) Jesus takes servanthood and raises it to a high place, as is expressed in this little poem.

Mother's Reward
(anon.)

You are the trip I did not take,
You are the pearl I can not buy,
You are my blue Italian Lake,
You are my piece of foreign sky,
You are my Honolulu moon,
You are the book I did not write,
You are my heart's unuttered tune,
You are a candle in my night,
You are the flower beneath the sun
In a dark sky a bit of blue,
Answering disappointment's blow
With, "I am happy! I have you!"

So, first we see mother as a *willing* servant, acting out of love. "Make me a servant, humble and meek"—give me a servant's heart, Lord. It's the highest position on Jesus' list.

Secondly, we see mother as a *wise* servant. A servant is around the people she serves. She spends time with them. She is the leader, perhaps not acknowledged, but the leader nonetheless.

Herman Hesse's story, *Journey to the East,* describes a band of men on a journey. The central figure of the story is Leo who accompanies the party as the servant. Leo does their menial chores, but he also sustains them with his spirit and his song. He is a person of extraordinary presence. All goes well until Leo disappears. Then the group falls into disarray and the journey is abandoned. They cannot make it without the servant, Leo.

The story teller, who is one of the party, after some years of wandering, is taken into the Order that had sponsored the journey.

There he discovered that Leo, whom he had first known as servant, was in fact, the head of the Order, its guiding spirit, a great and noble leader.

Is that you, Mom? Proverbs 31 speaks of the wife of noble character. It first tells of all the tasks she does; she works, provides, buys and sells, trades, sews, helps the poor. Then in verse 26, it says, "She speaks with wisdom, and faithful instruction is on her tongue." Moms, the way to become wise is to read God's word, the Bible, and to heed what it says. Mother as wise servant—influencing her family for good.

Finally we see mother as a *witnessing* servant. In our scripture lesson, Salome, the mother of disciples James and John, comes to Jesus requesting a favor for these two sons. She desires and requests personal success for them, prominence, "to sit on either side" of the king. To be honest, that's what most moms want for their children. We are ambitious for them.

But Jesus is facing the cross. We might say his kingdom, his success, is going to come from his suffering. His success is going to come out of defeat. Is that what Salome was thinking? I think not.

Jesus' answer was that those who would share his triumph must drink his cup. Out of the sorrow, struggle, and suffering, will come the victory. No mother wants to see her child suffer.

Mother, as servant, you have the tremendous ability to help bring beauty out of the ashes for your children. Life has its suffering and its struggles. You can help your children come out on the top side in what God sees as important. That should be your ambition. That is your witness.

Mom, do you have a handicapped child? No matter what that handicap is—physical, mental, emotional, social—that handicap requires more servanthood from you. That child requires more care, more time, more energy, more sacrifice, but that child also has the potential to show more of God's glory, more of God's power. The Bible tells us, "God chose the foolish things of the world to shame the wise; God chose the weak things of the world to shame the strong. He chose the lowly things of this world and the despised things—and the things that are not—to nullify the things that are, so that no one may boast before him." (1 Corinthians 1: 27-29)

I think that that's why there are handicapped people on this earth. God places them here so that his power can be seen more clearly in their weakness, in overcoming...whether in healing the handicapped—or higher yet, in spiritual victory over the handicap. Spirit is free! Spirit advances! People take note when they witness an "overcoming spirit" in a handicapped person.

The mom whose godly ambition is to guide her child (handicapped or not) through God's power, will indeed be a witnessing servant. When mom's attitude is positive and she relies on God, she is helping her children get through their troubles by fixing their eyes on Jesus.

Does this mean that mom will have to negate herself and be unfulfilled in her talents? Absolutely not. The God of the universe will find a time and a place for all her creativity to surface—in the home and in the larger community. The indwelling Holy Spirit gives gifts, "so that the body of Christ may be built up." (Ephesians 4:12) Jesus says," If you want to be great, be a servant; if you wish to be first of all, be a slave." That's revolutionary. That's a complete reversal of the world's standards. That's a complete new set of values.

Moms, your position in the family entitles you to be a servant.

Are you a willing servant?

A wise servant?

A witness of God servant?

May it be so, in Jesus name.

"Let your face shine on your servant." (Psalm 31:16)

Mama's Like a Pitman

Mama's like a pitman
          on the Indianapolis 500
   servicing the high speed fancy Formula 1 racers
making sure
   that all the parts are running, purring
    fueling up the gas tank
          making sure
            that no debris or
                imperfections remain
             to slow down
    the roaring, raring, racing, charging sleek machines

Mama's rushing down the
             grocery aisle
      tossing groceries
       into the cart
        with both hands
       making sure
        the food is

processed, pickled, canned, sautéd, chopped, diced, mashed,
fried, blanched, boiled, baked, and
thrown on the table for
the hungry executive and
ravenous teenagers
revving up their motors
anxious to refuel
and be on their way again
around
the dangerous curves and
high speed race track
of their lives

Mama's running
to the laundry
armloads full of soiled clothing
making sure
the clothes are
washed, dried, ironed, bleached, deodorized, softened,
fluffed, folded, stacked, and
all the stains removed
matching up 600 pairs
of white athletic socks
all with different stripes
whose mates are all hiding
wadded up
under the bed or lost
in some foreign locker room
making sure
the impatient cars are all
polished, washed, waxed, slicked, buffed,
patted, petted, soothed, shined, glistening, beautiful, and
ready to go
once more
roaring

another lap
around the challenging race track
of their lives

Mama's standing in a cloud of
dust
breathing the exhaust fumes
that are left behind
when all the racers
have roared out to lap
each other
side by side straining
to see which one
is fastest, bestest, mostest powerfulest, greatest
liveliest, daringest, bravest, winningest

making sure
that all the clutter oil cans, gas cans, grease rags,
wrenches, screw drivers, pliers, sockets, gauges, plugs, points
are picked up, cleaned off, and in their proper
places
ready

for tomorrow's race
on the
Indianapolis
Speedway

Memorial Day

I remember that 1968 Memorial Day clearly. The sky was bright and blue. A breeze was blowing. It made all the little red, white, and blue flags which had been placed on the soldiers' graves, flutter in the breeze. Here and there, dotted around the cemetery those flags stood straight, like brave little sentinels, guarding sacred ground.

The local Memorial Day scene was a familiar one. In my mind's eye I could see myself watching the high school marching band, preceded by uniformed veterans carrying the flag, making the trek to the cemetery. I could hear the muted drums "boom, boom" as the marchers entered the cemetery gates. I remember seeing the wreath carefully carried by a veteran, being laid on an honored gravesite, and hearing the speech by the local mayor. Then everyone bowed for the prayer by a clergy person from one of the village churches, and held their ears for the firing of the guns in military salute to those who had lost their lives defending our country, America. Then I imagined slowly walking with the townspeople to exit the cemetery to partake of holiday festivities, perhaps the first picnic of the season.

But this year was different. Suddenly the meaning of all this ritual clutched my heart. My brother Bob was in Viet Nam, fighting a war. One of these graves could very well be his. My heart welled up and anxious fearful thoughts flooded my mind. "Oh Bob, you are so young, only eighteen, and so brave and willing to do what is necessary. Will you be spared to return home? Will you live to march in a Memorial Day parade like this one?"

I stood there after the others had left and looked at the graves. Tears ran down my cheeks and I whispered a prayer for my brother. "Thank you God, that Bob is willing to fight for our country. Please protect him and bring him back. Amen."

"Be strong and courageous. Do not be afraid or terrified because of them, for the Lord your God goes with you...."
(Deuteronomy 31: 6)

That Memorial Day was truly a patriotic one for me. I knew without a doubt what love of country and willingness to sacrifice could mean. I thank God that my brother Bob did return.

In hindsight I question, is personal involvement or experience always necessary for us to understand events and to reverence those who are part of them? Perhaps not, but it does enable us to truly relate to the meaning of the events we memorialize.

On Patriotism

One April I had the privilege of attending a conference in San Antonio, Texas. It was festival time there, complete with a three-hour parade marching through the city, past the famous Alamo. As I watched part of the parade, I was struck not only with the joyful holiday atmosphere, the snappy uniforms, beautiful costumes, prancing horses, lively bands, and elaborate floats, but also with the show of patriotism that was displayed. When the American flag came by, followed by a regiment of soldiers from a nearby base, people stood up and cheered. Many people placed hands on their hearts and stood in reverence as Old Glory passed by. The red, white, and blue motif was present in decorations, flowers, costumes, and parade vehicles. America was proud. It was a good feeling to hear the cheers and see the display of patriotism. We northerners in our parades look pale, puny, and lukewarm in comparison.

Now, I know that patriotism is a lot more than flag-waving and cheers, so the whole scene made me think about love of country and willingness to die for one's country. That willingness is tied up in personal ownership of the land. We have invested ourselves in our country. We were born here, live here, go to school here, are raising our families here, go to church here and probably will die here. This is "OUR" country. We own it, and despite its faults, we love this land. Soldiers have fought and died for us to keep these privileges. That should be enough to stir our sluggish blood and fire us with patriotism.

But there needs to be another element. A deeper one. God and country go together. If God is not in it, no battle will have any meaning. Loss of life for a cause will not be glorious, but foolish. Mothers' sons will lie beneath the sod for no reason. That is unbearable.

The story of David and Goliath demonstrates a clear biblical view of patriotism (1 Samuel 17:26-51). David, the shepherd boy, is appalled that the Philistines, with their champion Goliath, are defying the ranks of Israel, the people of the living God. With great courage, David goes out to fight the giant Goliath. You know the outcome of the story. David triumphs over the giant with a slingshot stone to the forehead. His pronouncement rings out loud and true. *"The battle belongs to the Lord."*

The only battles worth dying for are the Lord's. How long has it been since our country cared about God and God's causes, deeply enough to die for?

Summer

" The wind blows wherever
it pleases..."
(John 3:8)

Brandy

"But ne'er the rose without the thorn" (From *The Rose,* by Robert Herrick). That line fits her. The thorn part, I mean. A rose draws its attention by its beauty, its fragileness, its perfume, perhaps its perfection. We only notice the thorn if we accidentally bump into it. It pricks. It scratches. We jump back. Ouch! Such a hurtful stem or vine to hold such a beautiful rose. "Rose,", why did you choose to hide behind your thorns?

The large clinic waiting room is crowded with people. She sits on the blue leather-looking plastic cushioned seat, waiting for a friend. Across two rows of people she spies someone she knows. "Hi Cindy!" she calls in a loud voice. "Haven't seen *you* in a long time. How's your little boy, whats iz name? The last time I saw you was at that New Year's Eve party. Remember how drunk Joe was? He's in jail now. How about your brother—ever get out of Gowanda? I heard he was over there. Yeah. I'm married now, did you know that? Yeah, I married a guy in prison. His name is Tony. We got married by the prison chaplain. Nobody else would marry us." She laughs.

The casual magazine readers in the room have stopped their reading. Ears prick up. Sly glances look to see who would marry a man already in prison. The audience is attentive, waiting.

"That your husband beside you?" she inquires.

"No."

"Oh, he's your boyfriend. Hi."

Now Brandy turns to a pregnant woman beside her with a broken leg.

"How'd ya break your leg?" The voice is still loud. "Yeah, I broke my foot when my kid was five months old. I had to go up and down stairs on my butt with the kid on my belly. Boom-ba-boom-ba-boom." She makes the motion to show how a short pudgy gal like herself managed it. Everybody laughs. She repeats the story and the motions. It gets laughs again.

On to another story, and another. The more painful the story, the more Brandy laughs. The funnier she makes it. "Tell ya about the cops down in the apartments last night? Pounding on the door at 2am. Woke Kathy up and she got all upset and bawled the rest of the night. Some dude told them that Mike was stayin at my place. He ain't here, I told 'em. If you wanta search my place, go ahead. I haven't got anything to hide. No? Then get your butt outta here."

A rose, by any other name still has thorns. Thorns are what you get. And if you want me, you get my thorns. "That's us Majors. We've always been tough. My dad would beat the crap out of anybody. Done it lots of times. To us kids, too. Pow-pow." She smacks a backhand, laughing. On and on it goes. Ugly adventure after ugly adventure. If the listener doesn't respond with enough shock then the next story will be uglier. "I got raped, you know...."

Brandy, Brandy, I can't stand it anymore! Somewhere under those thorns is a real rose—or was —or even a faded petal of one. Jesus can repair even a torn rose. But do you really want to let him? It's so much safer to be a thorn. Brandy has been a thorn all her life. It's how she survives.

"I laugh so that I can bear it," Brandy told me when I questioned her. Then in the next sentence, "Did I tell ya that Jim's with me now? His wife knows it too. They're getting a divorce. I wanted you to know because I'm not trying to hide anything. I figure its ok because

Tony says he's divorcing me anyways. Besides, I had to take Jim in. He had no place to go. His wife booted him out."

Brandy, stop! The thorns have pricked me too much. Blood is running down my arms. I offered you my Jesus, Brandy. You said you wanted him. I thought you really did, back there when you were sick. But you shunned him when you got better. I have to back away from you. The thorns are too painful for me. But I will always pray for the rose.

"Why do you boast of evil?" (Psalm 52:1)
"Trust in the Lord with all your heart and lean not on your own understanding."
(Proverbs 3:5)

Build Your House on the Rock

Therefore everyone who hears these words of mine and puts them into practice is like a wise man who built his house on a rock. The rain came down, the streams rose, and the winds blew and beat against that house; yet it did not fall, because it had its foundation on the rock.

But everyone who hears these words of mine and does not put them into practice is like a foolish man who built his house on sand. The rain came down, the streams rose, and the winds blew and beat against that house, and it fell with a great crash."

When Jesus had finished saying these things, the crowds were amazed at his teaching, because he taught as one who had authority, and not as their teachers of the law.

(Matt: 7:24-29)

Don't you like the way Jesus teaches? It's so clear and so easy to understand. He doesn't give a three hour lecture using million dollar words. He gives a clear picture—one to remember: a wise man building his house upon a rock, and a foolish man building his house upon the sand—and then a rain storm comes.

Jesus is speaking of the total person—body, spirit, and soul—using the house as a symbol. Modern psychologists agree that in our dreams a house stands for the total person. I had such a dream when I was in college. I went to college as an older adult, after 22 years basically at home. During that time, I kept having dreams about a house. I'd be in a house and there was all this old wallpaper peeling off. What should I do about it? The house was full of elaborate furniture someone had given us. I didn't like the furniture at all but I didn't know what to do with it. (Do you ever have dreams that you repeatedly dream and wonder what they're all about?)

My house—my life, was rapidly changing, and I was trying to combine the new with the old, symbolized by the old wallpaper and the new furniture. How could I arrange my "house": my self, my life— to make changes and still please others? My dream reflected the conflict I felt as I sought to make these changes. That's what had disturbed me. Understanding my dream helped me to get a perspective.

In Jesus' parable, the house, the total person, is to be built upon the *rock,* which Jesus identifies as *his* words, *his* teaching. A rock is solid, everlasting, firm, secure, true, a perfect base—nothing moves it, nothing destroys it! So, to truly build our whole person on the rock (Jesus' words), we must avail ourselves to what Jesus offers: himself and his kingdom. Then we will have his power to build upon his words. That's the first part of being the wise man. What a glorious thing to start building your house on the rock, and to know that it will stand!

Jesus says the storms come and beat upon the house. Isn't that the truth! Life seems to go along fine and then bam! You lose your job, or your spouse wants a divorce, or the lab test shows up cancer, or your son has to go to war. Life is hard on us all.

When we build our lives on the words of Jesus, we may still take a beating, but we will stand. We may grieve, and we may struggle, but we will not crumble, because Jesus is our solid foundation.

In contrast is the man who builds his house on the sand. He who builds his life on anything other than Jesus Christ is building on the sand. I remember that when our daughter, Char, was in the hospital for a stay, one afternoon she sat in the hall by a 75-year-old man. As she talked to him, he told her that his life was ruined. His only son had died 25 years before. "Life has never been the same," he said. Now he had serious physical ailments. He had lost his will to live. That was shocking to Char.

Some people build their lives on another person. Perhaps it happens on the wedding day when that wonderful man or woman is placed *highest up* in the other's life, taking the place of God. What happens when that one falls off their pedestal, which they surely will? We hear the cry, "You're not the person I thought you were." Disillusionment sets in. It happens most often with a spouse, but it can be a friend, a child, a parent, a mentor, a lover. When we allow any person to take the place of God in our lives, it is idolatry. Some day that person will reject, hurt, or disappoint us or even leave, abandon, or divorce us, and how can the house stand when that storm hits?

There are many forms of idolatry. What about the people who build their lives on their money? They feel secure—and then the stock market crashes. Winds of change are blowing. Or, those who build on their work and then they get too old to work. "I used to get up at 6am and work all day. Now I can't work at all." What about the people who build their lives on their children?—and then the kids grow up and move far away and they don't see them very often—the storm is beating on the house. That's why it's necessary to build on the rock—Jesus Christ. He will always give you a meaningful life.

We can even build a house on ourselves—superman. I don't need anyone else. I'm rough, tough —but what happens if an accident, disease, or old age comes along?

Or what about the people who build their foundation of trust on the government? Since the 9/11 attacks on the U.S., we haven't felt as secure. The winds of change have been beating upon us. Terrorists are a threat. We constantly hear from our leaders about the certainty of more attacks, or biological warfare, or possible nuclear attacks. They could keep us in a state of anxiety. The government can't protect us. Who will? Christ only. The Rock. All else is sand.

Maybe, like the foolish man who built his house on the sand, these people who built on other things did hear Jesus' words. The words sounded good—but they never put them into practice. They never seriously prayed, or cared about what Jesus said or followed his directions. They may have said they were Christians but they didn't practice it. They built their house according to their own self-will, on their own worldly desires. And then, "The wind blew and beat against that house and it fell with a great crash."

Maybe you are one of those persons whose house has fallen. Maybe you built your own house and it was no good, and it crashed. You are "poor in spirit." Jesus says, "Blessed are the poor in spirit." Why? Because you are ready to come to Christ, you are ready to learn, you are ready to be taught, ready to follow Christ. You are indeed blessed. There's nothing in the parable that says you can't rebuild or start over. In fact, if your house (life) has been totally leveled, you're in a position to start building. Pick up that first brick (the word of Jesus to you today) and place it on the rock. Make that commitment to Christ. You have nothing to lose and everything to gain.

And to those of you who have built your house on the rock—I say hallelujah! Your house will weather all the storms. You will be strong in the Lord.

Through a Sponsor's Eyes

My husband, Ron, and I are sponsors of a six-year-old girl in Haiti named Sophonie Noel. When I made arrangements to go on a VISA mission trip to Haiti in February, 1999 to work with J.R. and Becky Crouse, I inquired about the possibility of meeting Sophonie while I was there. I was excited when the answer was "yes." Sophonie lives in Dubedou, a village in northern Haiti, close to Mapou where the Crouses were stationed.

The big day arrived on a Sunday. After church, J.R., Becky, Haitian Pastor Delamy and I loaded into the small Toyota truck to go to Dubedou. Our dirt road got even bumpier and smaller as we rode through heavy brush and lush green foliage, down a gully, across a dried-up creek bed, and finally into an opening where a green stucco-cement church came into view. We got out and followed Pastor Delamy past the church, up a steep footpath, jumping over ditches and shooing scrawny goats out of the way, until we came to Sophonie's little two room house of baked mud, topped with a corrugated tin roof.

My heart was beating with anticipation. Now I was going to meet the little girl whose picture I posted on my refrigerator, and touched every day with a prayer. There she was, dressed in a pretty peach-

colored dress, bows in her jet-black hair, a shy smile on her face—
Sophonie. Standing with her was her mother holding her baby
brother, while three younger sisters huddled near.

It was a big occasion. Chairs were brought out for us to sit under
the shade of the extended roof. We exchanged smiles and words of
greeting interpreted by J.R., Becky, and the pastor. I had brought
some gifts: clothing, school supplies, dolls, and a scarf for her
mother. Sophonie sat on my lap the whole time and admired my gifts,
but did not run off to play. At first she didn't talk but suddenly she
started singing one of the songs she had learned at the Free Methodist
school she attends.

It was the dry season; no appreciable rain had fallen for four
months. Sophonie's father had gone off to the city of Port-au-Prince
to look for work.

A man brought coconuts and chopped off the husks with a
machete.

Under the watchful eye of the neighbors, we drank the coconut
milk, while the children, friends, and neighbors were served chunks
of coconut.

My heart twinged when I noticed two of Sophonie's sisters had
red in their otherwise black hair, a sign of malnutrition. I was glad I
had brought some money to give their mother for food.

Then it was time to go. Time to leave these beautiful people with
the big smiles and friendly ways. Tears filled my eyes. I had to say
good-bye to Sophonie. I kept looking back to wave as I went down
the path. Sophonie and Haiti are still in my heart. My life is forever
changed by this visit. I hope to return some day.

*"You will be made rich in every way so that you can be generous
on every occasion, and through us your generosity will result in
thanksgiving to God." (II Corinthians 9:11)*

The Prickly Cross

The words hurt. Did she know how much?
Lack of understanding shouted back at me.
Self-defense. Unkind comparisons.
I had to take it. With little answer. Even that
was not accepted. After that, a weariness.

So I went for a long walk, and called upon my
friend Jesus.
He put an arm around me. Comrade-style.
I talked and he listened.

His response was gentle
"Yes, it was a cross, the prickly kind," he said,
"Those can be miserable, can't they?"
He took it off me. It looked like coiled
wire with little prickers on it. He held it for
a moment and it vanished.
I smiled. "It's gone!"

Then I remembered that unkind comparison
she made about someone more loving and
more talented than me.
How my challenger loved that woman.
I didn't stack up. "That was a low blow, wasn't it?"
said Jesus, pulling the thorn out of my stomach.
He paused. Lightly he said, "Almost as painful as that
one you put in my crown."

In a flash, I saw his crown of thorns.
I didn't know whether to laugh or cry.
Yes, Jesus.
Forgive me. I forgive her.
We went on our way.

My Friend Barb

She was brought into the church by a woman who attended occasionally and who introduced her to me. "This is Barb. She's a client of my sister."

"Hi Barb," I said. "I'm Barb, too."

A client, what is a client? my mind momentarily wondered, and then she was gone. She was a big girl, a grown woman really, kind of lumbersome and slow, but with a child-like eagerness. Barb had inquired, "Kin I work in the nursery? I like kids!"

"Sure Barb, we always need nursery helpers," I replied. I didn't see Barb for quite a while after that, but eventually she started coming most every Sunday, and eventually she needed a ride to church, and eventually I was the one to pick her up, so eventually I got to know her. Barb lived in a Family Care home. Three other female clients lived there, too. It wasn't a bad place. Barb said it was the best place she had ever lived in.

"I love this schurch," she would say wistfully, and "I love you, Barbara. I wish I could be just like you." It was a little embarrassing but also touching. I didn't deserve such adoration. It isn't every day that someone shows us that kind of devotion.

Barb began to come to all the social things at church, and all the religious things and all the work things. If the church was open, she wanted to be there.

"Kin I be in the Youth Group? Kin I be in the Christmas play? Kin I do the opening at church? Kin I lead the song with you? Kin I come to Board meeting?" The answer would either bring a happy smile, and, "Hey, I'm gonna be in the Christmas play!" or a resigned, "Shucks."

Barb had spells. She'd come to the Adult Membership Class with her head drooping, chin almost on her chest. Her glasses hung down on her nose. Her dark brown hair hung over her eyes. She moved even slower.

"Hi. What's the matter Barb?"

"I miss my mommy so much," she would say, crying. The class members tried to comfort her. We'd hug her. We'd sympathize with her. We'd take her aside and pray for her. We'd reason with her. We'd encourage her. The lower lip still hung down. An hour would go by. The class time would be over. The planned lesson hadn't been taught. But we had comforted Barb. I wasn't entirely easy about it.

During church service Barb would make trips in and out. To the bathroom. To get water. To check out whatever. I talked to her about it. She stopped. At prayer request time Barb always raised her hand, "Pray for my sister, Nancy, and Sherry and Dave and Gerri, and a guy at the workshop, and his grandmother, and for Joe who got drunk and hit his girlfriend and swore." Barb always had people for prayer time.

New Year's Eve came. The church was having a watch-night service and party. People came for pizza and games. Kids were running around the fellowship room. Teens were laughing. Adults were kidding each other. Barb was moping, in the corner, head down. The word went out, call Pastor Barb. "You've gotta talk with Barb. She's having a bad night."

"Let's go pray, Barb," I said. I listened to her story. I spent time with her. I hugged her. I prayed. Barb continued to mope. She wanted me again. I was busy. There were thirty other people there, and a service to start. Then the cry went out. "Barb's run off." She'd left the church and was headed over the bridge and toward town. People ran out to find her—to bring her back. She came back reluctantly.

Barb sat in the back of the sanctuary during the service, crying. At the end I called her up front and we prayed for her. Her nose was running, unwiped. People were getting annoyed. I was getting annoyed. She had monopolized the whole evening. When she got home that night she was grounded for any evening activities. I was relieved. We all needed a break.

Later, the phone rang. It was Barb. "I'm not going to go to your schurch anymore. Nope. I was bad. I just don't want to go to your schurch anymore. Okay, good-bye." Then I felt bad. Several weeks went by. Then Barb came back. She apologized over and over for her New Year's Eve behavior.

"It's okay, Barb. I understand. We forgive you," I assured her.

Barb always had notes for me, notes expressing her love for me and for the church. She brought me coloring book pictures she had done and little gifts. She called me on the phone just to say "hi" and share the good news of her day. "Guess what, Pastor Barb? I'm gonna have three days at the workshop starting next week. Isn't that great!"

Summer came. Barb wanted to go up to the Christian camp for evangelistic services. Lots of people were there. My youth group was in and out of the cabin. Old friends came up for the day and for the evening services. There was talking and laughing and numerous activities. Barb was having trouble, tears, dejection, depression, self-pity. "I miss my mommy," she whined. I comforted, I hugged, I prayed, all to no avail. Annoyance began to arise in me.

"Barb, if all I did was dwell on all the bad things in my life, I'd cry all the time, too. But we can't do that. You're a Christian. You have the living Christ inside you. Stop thinking about all the bad things," I lectured her.

We walked on the trail around the camp. "See that woman over there? She's blind!" I went on, "She has every reason to feel terrible, but she doesn't cry. She helps the little kids make boon-doggles. Now I want you to stop crying."

The moping continued. I lost my patience. "That's it, Barb! If you don't shape up, I'm going to have somebody take you home, and I won't have you come up here again." Barb snapped out of her slump immediately. "Okay." she said in a normal voice. "I'll see you over at the service." I was amazed.

As she walked away I shouted, "And I want to see a smile on your face!"

Barb sat in the row behind me during the service. I turned around and the big grin on her face said it all.

Being sympathetic over all her laments and self-pity was only feeding the bad spirit that occupied such a stronghold in her life. From then on my firm stand against any unseemly whining, crying, and manipulating put an end to it.

People began to notice a difference in Barb. She got her hair permed, held her head up, and quit demanding center-front stage. My heart was touched on the Sunday she remembered my birthday and during the service presented me with a lovely statue of the holy family. No one else had remembered it.

At Bible Study or Prayer Circle, Barb often took her turn at praying. Everyone was moved by her Spirit-touched prayers. Short and childlike, a pure word or two seemed to come straight from God.

Time went by, and I transferred to another church. Barb and I still keep in touch by short letters. She always writes, "I love you very much, Barb!" I like that. It's good to know I still have my friend, Barb, same name as mine.

"But God has combined the members of the body and has given greater honor to the parts that lacked it." (1 Corinthians 12: 24)

Home from Haiti

On my return trip to the USA from the country of Haiti, where I had been working with a missionary couple for two weeks, I sat beside an elderly woman. She was a Haitian woman, humbly dressed, small and thin, her dark skin lined and wrinkled with age. As the plane roared down the runway for take-off, she raised her hands to heaven, praying in her native French Creole language. I, too, was praying for a safe ascent with hands folded and head bowed. We smiled at each other as we settled in our seats for the flight over the ocean to New York City. I thought how brave it was for an aged woman to be flying alone to a foreign country. I wondered if she might be visiting family members in New York City where there was a large Haitian community.

After a time the flight attendant came by and handed us forms to fill out. We pulled down our tray tables for a base on which to lay out the forms. The flight attendant offered to help my seat-mate fill hers out. I glanced at her form as she wrote and I had a feeling she glanced at mine. The first line was her name and then the second line was date of birth. The startling information she wrote on that line put her birth date in the same year as mine. This woman, whom I had estimated as twenty years my senior, was in fact my age.

I almost felt embarrassed. Here I was, a privileged woman from the richest country in the world. By my country's standards, if I lived the national average life span, I could expect 15 or 20 more years, while she was already past the average Haitian life span of 57 years. Well-nourished, strong, educated, working a job which demanded the energy I had to give, blessed by a good husband and family, living in a nice home with every modern convenience I could want, backed up by readily available medical services, assured of financial stability when old age came, I was indeed one of the privileged of the world.

In contrast this woman, who so dearly trusted the Lord on take-off, lived in a country where famine reached out its bony fingers at any given time. Even in good times there was not quite enough to eat. Her house might have been one of the many mud huts with tin roofs of the countryside. If the capital city of Port-au-Prince had been her home, she might have been one of the million people who lived crowded into small old buildings with sporadic electricity and no plumbing, where sewage ran down gullies in the crowded hillside streets. Perhaps she was like the Haitian woman who worked for the missionaries part time; helping with cooking, cleaning, and laundry, earning income which made her the sole support of sixteen family members.

My mind flashed back to the crowded airport I had just left. At the entrance men had lined the sidewalks by the dozens reaching our their hands and indicating that they would like to carry your suitcases—the one chance that would earn them a few coins to buy bread for supper.

Shrunk back in my seat, I felt ashamed—ashamed that I'd ever been annoyed over tiny inconveniences—ashamed that I'd been fussy over the color of the new curtains—ashamed for 101 petty things that made up the trappings of my existence while this woman and her loved ones, living in the poorest country in the western hemisphere, struggled to survive. Tears stung in my eyes as they had so many times in the past two eye-opening weeks.

Life is so unfair, I thought. With shock I questioned whether my privileged lifestyle somehow perpetuated that unfairness. Next to her I felt pampered and unworthy. What could I do, send relief money? Yes, but somehow it didn't seem sufficient. I could give away all my material goods but would causing my family to suffer solve the problems of Haiti?

The Bible calls us to weep with those who weep and rejoice with those who rejoice. How could I suffer with them? I could suffer in my prayers and in my tears. I could preach it, and make others understand what I now saw so clearly. We are indeed responsible for these people. We are our brother's keepers. We Americans have the best land and the world's largest share of resources, can we not sacrifice even a little to help? So many people in America are apathetic. Giving personal help doesn't really seem necessary to them because our country gives billions to other nations.

The red sun had set and now in the darkness we could see the spectacular lights of New York City stretching out as far as the eye could see. Home at last. In the airport my heart thrilled to the attendant's smile and words, "American citizen," and his outstretched arm indicating for me to go to his right. With a more severe look, he spoke to the many Haitians and ushered them into a long line at his left, for aliens. They must wait.

I was once more on my way, taking a two hour flight that would get me home. Relieved and anxious to see my husband, I turned my thoughts toward him and pondered how to share my experiences and my burden with him and with my church. I would never be the same.

My husband and I would send money to help the hospital in Dessalines, Haiti, and our church would help to support our missionaries there. I breathed a prayer, "Lord, never let me forget Haiti and let me be faithful to do what I can."

"Suppose a brother or sister is without clothes and daily food. If one of you says to him, 'Go, I wish you well, keep warm and well fed,' but does nothing about his physical needs, what good is it?" (James 2:15,16)

Day by Day

"O Dear Lord—three things I pray:
To see Thee more clearly
To love Thee more dearly
To follow Thee more nearly
Day by day."

So sang the lively group of young people portraying modern-day disciples following Jesus, in the Broadway musical and movie *Godspell*. This was sung in the 70s, but the thought has always stayed with me. Day by day.

The idea of "daily life" has about it a slow, steady pace i.e. the daily paper, daily devotions, a daily walk, the daily dozen, our daily bread, the daily grind, daily work, etc. Our daily rituals, whatever they may be, seem mundane; the same old thing.

Many of us crave an exciting life—adventure, romance, achievement, emotional high, newness —you name it. Certainly the media, which has such influence, fosters the whiz-bang life. Daily stuff is seen as b-o-r-i-n-g.

And yet the "daily" life was given to us by God as a means to promote purpose, thoughtfulness, depth of character, stability, peace and gratefulness for the little joys. It gives us time to think, to pray, to enjoy nature, and most of all – to meet with God. It gives us time to see and understand Him more clearly—to love Him more dearly (love grows with knowledge)—to follow Him more nearly, one step at a time. Day by day.

Sure, we like a little spice in life now and then, and God provides for that too. But most of life is meant to be steady. Think of Moses' forty years in the wilderness. And Jesus' thirty unknown years before his ministry began.

Americans have been called a people who live for the weekend. What happens the other five days? Focusing on what's ahead can rob us of what we're supposed to be learning and enjoying today. Consider the prophet Isaiah's words:

"In quietness and confidence shall be your strength." (Isaiah 30:15)

Today is looking better already.

Little Girl, Four-Years-Old

Little girl, four-years-old
I love you so.
Questions come—one on the other
Where is God?
Do people wear clothes up in heaven?
Will the babies in Heaven get bigger and grow up?
What would happen if you poured pickle juice
on the ground?

Little girl—trying to decide
if she is big or little
Walking carefully—trying not to spill the water for her
gerbil. Concentrating on putting it in his cage
Cutting out paper dolls—difficult work not to
gouge into the paper lady's arm. Oh now I've
cut her arm off and she's all ruined.
Tears and sobs.

Baby talk is fun to do.
See, I'm a baby…goo-goo, ga-ga
Mommy says "Cut out
that silly baby talk."
Little girl, whirling around the room
to the music, face aglow, raptured look
off in some unknown land
where grown-ups never go.

Wrestling with her brother
riding on his horsey-back
Oops, he bucked me off
and hurt my elbow
See that awful red mark
tears and sobs
Will it ever go away?
Little girl—four-years-old
Sit on mommy's lap
We'll sing the songs
and read the words and look at all the pictures.
Putting on a snowsuit is the hardest thing to do
And boots are even worse
They never go on right, even if you pull
And mommy shouts, "Now work on it! You're big
enough to do your own!"

Giggling at the table
the food is all so funny
and Russell eats it in a funny way
I can't help laughing
Even when Daddy gets mad and yells, "Stop it or
you'll leave the table."
Little girl, four-years-old.
I love you so.

On "Self"-Esteem

A while back I was at my daughter's house when my teenaged grandson came storming in. His anger was over a teacher in school, who in correcting him, "damaged his self-esteem," he said. According to him this was a "no-no" since his self-esteem was of the utmost importance. I raised my eyebrows, kept my mouth shut, and mentally added the incident to the growing mound of emphasis, perhaps over the last decade, on "Self"-esteem. Where do we get the idea that we are entitled to "Self"-esteem?

The biblical view of mankind is that we are a fallen race. We can in no way stand before a holy God on our own. We are darkened in our understanding, deceitful in heart and our entire moral and intellectual nature is corrupted by—yes—sin! We are desperately in need of a savior. Hence the need of repentance; hence the need of Jesus Christ for forgiveness of sins.

On our own we *should* have low "self" esteem, because it is a normal state of our being as natural man. Inherently, we realize our lack of perfection and our great need. To try to build self-esteem in our children simply because low esteem of self causes insecurity, misery and poor performance and because high self-esteem may give us a high-performance child misses the point. Such manufactured self-esteem will bottom out when a crisis occurs and "self" get the rug pulled out from under him/her.

What we need is "God" esteem. That occurs when we acknowledge our great need, turn to Christ in repentance, asking forgiveness, and receive the infilling of His Holy Spirit. Then begins the process of rebuilding us to be the persons that God intended us to be in the first place. As we work through the hardships, trials, troubles and struggles, as well as our daily routine, with God, following his commands, we develop good character. Our good character then, is the basis of our self-esteem. It is developed in us by God, who works in us to His good pleasure.

Parents who train up their children in this way, to be people of good character, will have given them the proper basis for esteem. Think about it. Is our esteem based on puny, self-serving "self" or on the strength that God develops in our inner person? Let's not jump on the bandwagon of every popular idea the psychology-sociology experts espouse, but instead, let's look deeper into what God says. We want "God" esteem.

Camaraderie

In 1953, Ron and I found ourselves in Condon, Oregon, population 400, surrounded by acres and acres of wheat fields. Having no vehicle, we had traveled by train, from Biloxi, Mississippi. A courier from the U.S. Air Force radar station drove twenty miles to the train station to transport us to the middle of town with our two suitcases and two cardboard boxes containing everything we owned. We gathered up our meager belongings and walked over to the town's only short-order restaurant and soda bar.

Inside, we met a friendly gal working there, whose husband was stationed at the nearby radar squadron where Ron was to sign in. She invited us to stay overnight with them, as there was no place to stay except a run-down hotel. Besides, we had spent all our money for train tickets to get us there, and wouldn't be reimbursed for a month. The next morning our newfound friends left for work, telling us to help ourselves to whatever we wanted for breakfast.

At lunch time, she returned and took us to look at a house in town available to rent. It was a tiny place; actually a converted chicken coop. We took it and were glad. It was all there was. Our month's rent would cost over a week's pay. Our money was gone so we went to the local grocery store, got an order, and asked to charge it (a common practice back then and one often done in our hometown where everybody knew everybody). The grocery owner shocked us by saying that he was sorry but we couldn't charge there. He had been burned by too many airmen who were shipped out and never paid him. We humbly put all the groceries back on the shelves, and wondered what to do (no credit cards back then).

Our newfound Air Force friends, Ray and Sue, came to our rescue again and loaned us some cash for groceries. They helped us clean the tiny rental house, invited us for supper, and oriented us to that little place, 3000 miles away from home.

In two months Ron was transferred and we started all over in Spokane, Washington. As in Oregon, other airmen and their wives came forth and helped us out. It wasn't long before we were in a group of friends who passed around maternity clothes, baby clothes, baby baskets and cribs, short-term loans and rides to work at the base for someone with a broken-down car. We took care of each other's children when a new baby arrived or when someone was sick. We all got together on Saturday nights to play cards, babies and toddlers included since no one could afford a babysitter.

All of us were in the same boat: young, far from home, a minority group (military families), temporarily poor, wondering who would be next to be shipped off to the Korean War. It was a time of true camaraderie; one that I have not experienced to such an extent since.

Necessity added to caring seems to create camaraderie. The closest we come to it in the Christian community is in our Small Groups. Whether Sunday night, or Wednesdays or any time a few gather, there is a likelihood of developing true camaraderie. I guess in the Christian community we call it "fellowship." Whatever it is, it's good! Jesus said, "Love one another as I have loved you." We see it in his closeness to his best friends, Peter, James and John, Martha and Mary and Lazarus. Let's not miss the opportunity to develop and experience this kind of fellowship.

"Let us not give up meeting together, as some are in the habit of doing, but let us encourage one another...." (Hebrews 10:25)

Human Pride

Our ancestors, Adam and Eve, took upon themselves the status of little "gods" when they disobeyed God and ate of the forbidden fruit in the Garden of Eden. Eve relied on her own judgement, therefore considering it to be more trustworthy than the very word of God. She rationalized that the fruit was good for eating, looked lovely, and would result in a beneficial outcome—the gaining of wisdom. Adam went along with his wife and he also ate, showing agreement with her logic, rather than standing on the specific instructions that God had given him.

The prophet Obadiah warns that, "The pride of your heart has deceived you" (Obadiah 3). The result was mankind's falling away from God.

Today we are still beset by this sin of pride. It shows itself when we act to "save face" rather than humble ourselves to ask forgiveness, when we insist on being right all the time, when we see ourselves as being a bit superior to others, when we follow our own ideas and desires rather than seeking God's will, when we live as if God's word doesn't apply to us.

We are all tempted by this subtle sin of pride. The Bible says, "No temptation has seized you except what is common to man. And God is faithful; he will not let you be tempted beyond what you can bear. But when you are tempted, he will also provide a way out so that you can stand up under it." (I Corinthians 10:13) How does Jesus teach us to escape?

"Take the lowest place." (Luke14:10) (not the place of honor)

"Wash one another's feet...no servant is greater than his master." (John 13:14,16)

Forgive. "I tell you...you must forgive him not seven times, but 77 times." (Matthew 18: 21,22)

Humble yourself. "For whoever exalts himself will be humbled, and whoever humbles himself will be exalted." (Matthew 23:12)

Sometime, ask your spouse, or an honest friend if you are acting out of humility or out of pride. You may not want to hear the answer, but it is one way of checking on whether prideful self is making the decision. This war against our human pride is an ongoing struggle. We are better equipped against it when we realize it as the truth, and then take the steps to combat it.

Remember, "the battle belongs to the Lord" and the Lord always wins. God will help you.

Smile. We'll lick the devil on this one yet.

Reconciliation

For Christ's love compels us, because we are convinced that one died for all, and therefore all died. And he died for all, that those who live should no longer live for themselves but for him who died for them and was raised again.

So from now on we regard no one from a worldly point of view. Though we once regarded Christ in this way, we do so no longer. Therefore, if anyone is in Christ, he is a new creation; the old has gone, the new has come! All this is from God, who reconciled us to himself through Christ and gave us the ministry of reconciliation: that God was reconciling the world to himself in Christ, not counting men's sins against them. And he has committed to us the message of reconciliation. We are therefore Christ's ambassadors, as though God were making his appeal through us. We implore you on Christ' behalf: Be reconciled to God. God made him who had no sin to be sin for us, so that in him we might become the righteousness of God. (11 Corinthians 5: 14—21)

❖

If your brother sins against you go and show him his fault, just between the two of you. If he listens to you, you have won your brother over. But if he will not listen, take one or two others along, so that every matter may be established by the testimony of two or three witnesses. If he refuses to listen to them, tell it to the church; and if he refuses to listen even to the church, treat him as you would a pagan or a tax collector. (Matthew 18: 15—17)

When I was a girl in high school I didn't get along well with my father. I didn't agree with most everything he said, and I argued my point—often making him angry. I was often angry at him. Now, when I had been a little girl, things had been different. I felt like I was "Dad's girl"—there are pictures of me happily sitting on his lap. But somewhere in Jr. High, Dad and I began to clash.

My Dad was the high school principal. Instead of being proud of his position, I agonized over that fact. In those days, the principal was the *disciplinarian,* and being sent to the principal's office meant that you were in big trouble. Needless to say, my Dad was not too popular, especially with the boys. He was an authority figure to be rebelled against. Because my friends were "all important" to me I tried to escape being labeled "the principal's daughter." (I remember one girl saying to me, "Oh, you're the principal's daughter—you must get everything you want!"). Yeah.

My dad would stand up in the school assembly and expound on how much more important academics and education were than sports. (After all, you couldn't earn your living in sports.) I took his words as a personal slam because my boyfriend, Ron Mosher, was an athlete and a star football player. Football was the school's most important team. Sports seemed to be everything in our small school.

After many years of hindsight I realize that Dad was just trying to build up the academic program —but I took it as a personal put-down.

Dad always wanted me to get the best grades and be the top student in my class, but I was interested in friends and resented the pressure. I got good grades, but he was always pushing me to do better than the school genius. In comparison to her I felt I was a disappointment to Dad. Resentment grew in me and I drew away from him. There was a rift between us.

Some years went by. Ron and I got married after high school and started our large family. I saw Dad at holidays—but I always kept him at arms' distance. Then, when I was 23 and Dad was 49, he had a heart attack, very unexpectedly. He was in an oxygen tent, and back in 1959 the doctors didn't have the technology and surgical processes they do now. You just had to wait it out. Dad was in bad shape.

We rushed up to the hospital, and everybody told me, "Dad wants to talk to *you.*" So I went in and sat by his bed. He was struggling to breathe. I was scared. Our eyes met. For a moment there was silence, then he said, "Barb, I'm sorry." I held his hand and choked up. I whispered, "I'm sorry, too, Dad." We looked into each other's eyes. There was pain there and there was forgiveness. There was love. It shone through. Our old disagreements melted away. My dad died the next day.

As grief-stricken as I was, as filled with remorse as I was that I never really knew Dad as an adult, there was a wonderful relief that we had forgiven each other. It was a blessed relief.

Later I pondered, *What if I had gotten there too late? What if I had had to go through life with the terrible burden, that out of my own stubbornness I had never told Dad I was sorry? What if we had never forgiven each other?* I am eternally grateful that God spared me that.

Forgiving is probably the most important thing we do in our lives. If we take the name of Christ and call ourselves Christians, then we have to realize that the greatest thing that Christ did, the greatest thing that Christ stood for, was reconciliation. He was and is the reconciler between us flawed human beings and God. "Father, forgive them."

"All this is from God, who reconciled us to himself through Christ."

I don't care if you are a great teacher, a great preacher, if you give all your money, sing with the voice of an angel, or are a tireless church worker, if you help all kinds of people. If you harbor unforgiveness in your heart, you are not following Christ and what he is all about. The message of Christ himself is forgiveness and reconciliation.

"If anyone is in Christ he is a new creation. The old has gone, the new is come!"

Forgiveness means pardon. If you are forgiven you are pardoned. The slate is cleared. But reconciliation takes the next step— reconciliation means to be friendly again, to be brought back to harmony. It's a *thoroughly changed* relationship.

11 Corinthians 5:18 could read literally: "all this is from God who thoroughly changed our relationship to himself through Christ, and made us ambassadors; entrusting the message of this radical change to us."

Now, how does that changed relationship work itself out? In my case, if my father had lived, reconciliation would have meant a changed relationship. We would have had to work at it. Reconciliation isn't easy. But with forgiveness to start it, you're three-fourths of the way there.

Reconciliation is not just being accommodating to somebody's faults. It is getting God's viewpoint. Since reconciliation is God's will and Jesus' ministry, the wisdom and power to reconcile are going to flow down from God through us. We will be able to reconcile because first our thinking will change, and then our doing will change.

Consider, what it would be like if there was real reconciliation between blacks and whites, between Christians and Muslims, between Israelites and Palestinians. Now you may say, "Preacher, you're getting too deep! I don't want to get into all that. I'm no good at this reconciliation stuff." I say to you, "Don't back off. Christ will guide you. He will send somebody into your life to help you."

The place to start is to be reconciled to God, through Christ. Sometimes we're angry with God, or don't quite trust God, or we're tied up with sin. That's why reconciliation with God is needed first. Surrender to God for your own healing and restoration. Surrender your own thoughts, so that they can be replaced by God's thoughts. Surrender your own will, so that God can empower you to be reconciled with Him, and then with others.

God wants our relationship with him to be friendly. God wants our relationship with him and with all other persons to be in harmony. Here's where real Christianity starts. We have nothing to lose—except our stubbornness—and everything to gain.

May God bless you as you take these steps toward reconciliation.

Living for Pleasure

Someone has said that Americans are, "lookers-forward-to-the-weekend-ers."

Work through the week, we might, but it's our weekends we really live for. The weekend is a time for our pleasure, whatever it may be: golfing, tennis, watching TV, Saturday night parties, sleeping in late, going visiting, going out to eat, catching up on yard work, you name it. Our focus is on our "free time" for pleasure.

In fact, part of the present American dream includes entering that time of life when we can retire, and spend all our days, or at least most of them, living for our pleasure. Days of travel, no alarm clocks, fancy vacations, doing our own thing, pursuing our hobbies, and supposedly enjoying our life (for a change?). Life can be fully focused on our pleasures, at last! We won't even have to feel guilty about committing hedonism, because after all, we earned it. We worked hard all those years. But there's something terribly wrong about this concept. And in our hearts we know it. To live focused on our pleasure is to die. Our spirit can't take it.

I remember my grandfather, who died when I was a little girl. He and my grandmother and eight children (my father was second to the youngest of the children) came to America, the land of opportunity, in 1912. They worked hard running a hotel. Grandma did all the cleaning.

When grandma died grandpa took it hard. He went to live with his daughters. Grandpa wanted to have a garden. His daughters; my aunts, wouldn't hear of it. "No Pa! You've worked hard—you deserve to rest. Come here, Pa, sit on the stoop. Sit on the stoop and rest." He did. Within six months he was gone. You've seen it happen. Time and again. The human spirit was meant to strive, to work, and not only for self and family, but for others.

Jesus tells the story of the rich man who had such a good crop that his barns wouldn't hold it all. So he decided to build bigger barns in order to store all his grain and other goods. (It sounds like a good retirement nest egg.) "Then I can say to myself, 'I have enough good things stored to last for many years. Rest, eat, drink, and enjoy life!' But God said to him, 'Foolish man!' Tonight your life will be taken from you. So who will get those things you have prepared for yourself?' This is how it will be for those who store up things for themselves and are not rich toward God." (Luke 12:16-21)

The world is full of misery, pain and suffering. Two thirds of the world's people go to bed hungry. And we focus on our pleasure! Retirement-age people have resources, life experience, understanding, wisdom, capabilities, know-how, and time. A crying world needs you. Tear down those barns, opt to get out of your comfort zone, look around, and offer yourself and your resources to God. He'll find a place for you. And life will be worth living.

They Marched into My Life

They marched into my life
   dancing feet
      prancing feet
         whirling, twirling, tiptoe
            sweaty, athletic sneaker feet and
            little baby piggy toes
            skipping hop scotch step-on-a-crack feet
   cuddly feet
   snuggly feet
      stroking joking provoking feet
            wobbly high-healed glitter feet
         dainty graceful slender arches
      leather booted riding feet
         running, jogging, leaping, high jump
                           triumphant
bruising, crying, blistered, slivered, swollen, soaking feet
      demanding feet
         haughty feet
            screaming tantrum naughty feet

dirty feet
  bare feet
    dusty, rusty, untrusty feet
        muddy, squishing, puddle-sloshing
          toe-pinching, form-fitting, sexy feet
          orthopedic corrective serviceable
                              ugly
roller feet
  ice skate feet
      cleat ski boot white buck clod-hopper
                          tennis feet
                      black patented leather
                      buckle foot
                    white bootie
                  pink bootie
                blue bootie
              leopard slipper
              cowboy boot
            rubber frog feet
  crashing
    dashing
      smashing
        laughing
    tramping
    chasing
        shouting
          racing
            stomping
              stamping
              kicking
                tricking
                raring
                  tearing
                    stampeding feet

STOP! STOP!

they retreated
about-face feet
sorry feet
grownup, hairy, vainglory feet
college feet
wedding feet
silk and satin and thong sandal
solemn feet
determined feet
honored diploma trophied feet
independent important feet
traveling, hiking, testing, hurrying,
stretching, earning, working feet
fly-away feet
glide-away feet
soaring
roaring
heel-clicking
toe-tapping
going going

WAIT
come back, I'm lonesome
Don't forget to march back into my life once in a while.
I miss you.

"How beautiful…are the feet of those who bring good news."
(Isaiah 52:7)

Earl Vaughn

He was an old man, in his nineties. His name was Earl and he lived in a hospital nursing home. As a nurse's aid, I liked having Earl assigned to me as a patient. He had been a farmer and knew a lot about growing things. If you could get through to him, he had very helpful answers to your questions.

I shouted in his good ear, "Earl, why aren't my tomato plants growing good?"

"Eh?" was the reply. I got up closer, with my mouth almost on his ear and repeated the question. "Where ya got 'em planted?" came his question.

"In the back yard," I shouted back.

After several other inquiries, he asked, "Near any trees?"

"Well, not too near, but there is a black walnut tree not too far away." Now he had the answer.

"That'll do it. Black walnut trees'll kill' em."

Earl was a wiry little man. Another aid and I would pick up his bent and arthritic body and put him in his geri-chair to be wheeled out to the dining room for supper. On the ride down the hall he would always lament, "May as well die and go to hell."

Other aids would kid with him and say, "At least you'll be warm there, Earl."

He told me that his mother had been visiting him lately. She came several times and stood at the foot of his bed. I wondered if his departure would be soon.

One evening when another aid and I were getting him ready for bed he again remarked that he might as well die and go to hell. I shouted, "Earl, wouldn't you rather go to heaven?"

"Eh?" was the answer. I made more effort to be heard. His reply was, "Don't know if they'll have me."

Earl, I shouted, "If you love God, if you're sorry for what you've done wrong…"

The other aid shouted, "If you accept Jesus as your Savior, you'll go to heaven."

Earl pondered this a minute and then responded, "That all there is to it?"

"Yup," we answered. That was all there was to the conversation. Earl made no more comments on going to hell. About two weeks later, I heard that Earl Vaughn had died while sitting peacefully in his geri-chair after supper. The aide went to wheel him back to his room, but he was gone. I expect that his mother had come to get him, and ushered him into heaven.

"Believe in the Lord Jesus, and you will be saved." (Acts 16:31)

Lesson in the Rockies

After 30 hours of riding in a cramped van, it was wonderful to stop in Allenspark, Colorado. Here, our youth group would enjoy three days of camping en route to an international youth convention. Several hikes were planned for that afternoon. After a quick lunch, our 31 students and 12 chaperones divided into different groups and off we all went. The group I was in tore off up the path, an eight mile hike, to view the scenery and to see a waterfall.

It was a gorgeous day. The bright blue skies, fluffy white clouds and majesty of the Rocky mountains made my body, mind, and spirit come alive. I was ready to go. But my body very soon got out of breath. The high altitude and my lack of training for this event made its mark quickly. However, I over-ruled the warning signs and pushed on.

Finally my body spoke to me, "Stop! Stop and rest! Or I'm going to quit on you." Finally my brain got the message.

"Okay, body, pace yourself. Slow down." I joined the tortoise group with Natalie and Kayla, and we made it all the way there and back. Slow and steady wins the race. When we returned, the others had long since left, but they sent a vehicle back to the finish area to pick up the three of us.

Later on I got thinking, some day our bodies will quit on us, for good. They'll simply wear out and stop working. Some day our minds will quit, hopefully not before the rest of our body does. But our spirit never quits. The spirit lives on and on after the body has faded away. That's why we need to pay so much attention to our spirit here, strengthening and nourishing it; acknowledging whence it came, and to whom it belongs.

Then when our body gives way, our spirit will go in free flight back to the Creator, back to join Jesus, back to that pure light. It will go the way we have directed it all the years of our lives. It will either go back to the Creator, or it will go to a place of eternal darkness.

Does your spirit know the way? Jesus said, "I am the way, the truth and the life. No one comes to the Father except through me." Jesus is that pure light that leads us to eternal life. On a rocky mountain high God made it real to me.

Autumn

"... bright as the skies
after the wind has swept
them clean"

(Job 37:21)

Who is Serving Whom?

Recently at a pastors' retreat, a question was given the pastors to reflect upon concerning servanthood. Usually an ordinary question, this one had a whole different slant. It concerned Christ's serving *us*. The question read, "Do you have any sense of Christ's wanting to serve you in some way? Any willingness on your part to let Him?"

How would you have answered that? For my self it was a radical idea. Of course I am very aware of God's blessings and grateful for them. But I am awed by Christ's serving me like he served the disciples by washing their feet. (John 13: 4-9) It's amazing to think of Christ serving us. We don't deserve it, for sure, and like Peter, would say, "No, you shall never wash my feet." It would be most awkward to have Christ show up in person and insist on doing some menial personal task for us. And yet he does, because "Jesus Christ is the same today, yesterday, and forever." (Hebrews 13:8)

Maybe he is the nurse's aid who brings you the bedpan at the hospital, or the man at the gas station who pumps your gas. Maybe he's the neighbor who bakes you some cookies, or the garbage man who picks up your trash. Or the person who pushes your stuck car out of the snow or fixes your flat tire. It could be the clerk who nicely explains how you filled out a form incorrectly and offers to help you fill it out right. Perhaps he's the child who sings you a song. The list goes on and on of servers who are "Christ," serving in disguise.

You may be one of them—a good server. But are you a good receiver? Are you accepting and grateful for the "Christ" who serves you in this way through somebody else? Do you gratefully acknowledge, "Christ" served *me* in this person or situation today?

Christ's service to us is a humbling experience. Especially for those who would rather be listed as servers. Maybe we can think of it as a circle. Christ serves us through unlikely people and in turn we are the unlikely people to serve others, as Christ.

Somebody just served me by giving me some nice tulip bulbs to plant for next year. Oops! I need to remember, "Christ just did that thoughtful deed through her." Thank you. Amen.

Letter to Amanda

Dear Amanda,

Your mother requested that I write about the events of your birth. And so I shall. It happened that your "birth mama" was not feeling too good and thought that you might soon be born. So she came to spend the night at our house, as I was the one who would be driving her to the hospital.

At about 3:00 in the morning (actually in the middle of the night), she woke me up saying that it was time to go!

We quickly got dressed and left for the hospital. The night was very dark, with a little rain and fog. She decided to ride in the back and lie down as it was quite a long ride to the hospital. There was music on the car radio which she requested be turned up loud.

As we were driving along your "birth mama" cried out, "Oh, I've had my baby! Barb, I've had the baby. Help me!"

Quickly I pulled the car over and stopped. I jumped out and ran around to open the back door of the car. But the inside light didn't come on so I couldn't see anything in the dark. I ran back around and opened my front car door wide. That made the light come on.

Then I saw you. You were lying face down on the seat of the car. I didn't know if you were alive. I picked you up by the feet and ankles and held you upside down as I had seen the doctors do in delivering a baby. I knew you had to cry because that would mean that you had started breathing.

I patted my hand up and down your back, giving you little spanks, all the while saying, "Cry, little baby cry, come on, cry! I was scared. You didn't show any signs of breathing. In desperation I called out, "Help us, Jesus! Help us!" Then you began to cry. How wonderful that sounded! I knew you had life. Your life in this world had begun.

All this time in the back of my mind was the realization that I was delivering James' and Susan's baby. So in that way your mother and father were there at your birth.

Wondering what to do about your cord I took my shoelace out of my sneaker and tied it around the cord. I wrapped you up in a big quilt that I had brought along in the car, and we went on our way to the hospital. I was so grateful I kept saying, "Thank you God, thank you God."

From the moment you were born you were special to me, as I know you are special to God and to your mother and father. Your "birth mama" cared about you, and wanted a good life for you. She chose me to find good parents for you who would love you and bring you up as a Christian. In turn, God helped me choose Susan and James as your parents.

The best thing is that God loves us all and helps us all. The Bible tells us: *"And we know that in all things God works for the good of those who love him, who have been called according to his purpose."* *(Romans 8:28)*

I hope that this letter helps you understand the events of your birth.

Your good friend,
Pastor Barb

Because I Said So

She came up to me after the Sunday morning worship service with a worried look on her face. The mother of three school-aged children, she herself had grown up in the church and she and her husband had faithfully attended this rural church all their married life.

Her request was that she needed to talk to me, so we went into my office. In an agitated voice she blurted out her concern. How did she know that she was really saved? How did she know *for sure* that she was going to heaven? The tone of her voice indicated that she wasn't going to take an easy answer and pat on the back.

I picked up a Bible and asked her if she believed this book was the revealed word of God. "Well, yes," was her guarded answer. Then I looked up the scriptures and read to her about confessing her sins, accepting Christ as her Savior and sincerely asking forgiveness in Jesus' name. "Well, I know all that," she said, "I know what the Bible says. But how do I know *for sure?*"

What she needed was personal assurance, and although I gave it to her she needed it directly from God. I prayed with her that God would give that assurance to her heart. She left my office with a rather unhappy look on her face. I took a deep breath and hoped for the best.

About six weeks later she came into church on a Sunday morning with a radiant look on her face. She had found an answer. The Lord had given it to her and she wanted to tell about it at the worship service. I made a place in the service for her to give her testimony and she came up front and told the congregation her story.

She had been sitting out on the back steps of her house one afternoon. Her children came out and began to beg her to take them downtown. "No," was her answer. They had been downtown a few days earlier and she wasn't going to take them again. They began to badger her with all kinds of explanations about why they just had to go. Her refusals were landing on deaf ears. Finally, in exasperation, she gave her firm final answer to their question why. Loudly and clearly she said, "Because I said so."

Suddenly, she said, the sky seemed to open on that cloudy day and she perceived those words coming back to her from heaven. "Because I said so." Hallelujah! What she so desperately had wanted to know about being saved and about heaven was answered directly from God. God's word was true. Now she knew it in her heart, *for sure,* because God said so!

"For the word of God is living and active." (Hebrews 4:12)

A Mistake?

It happened when we were on a mission trip to Ukraine. Five adults and five students from our church were working with missionaries there to provide an English Camp. During our two week stay an opportunity came up to visit an orphanage outside the city.

Imagine an old European orphanage. The old foreboding looking buildings set on a hill were enough to scare anyone away. Once inside, a bad smell assaulted your nose. The musty smelling, high-ceiling rooms had ancient wallpaper peeling from the walls. We carefully traversed a board across one hallway floor to keep from falling down where the floor had given away. Each large bedroom held eight or twelve small cots, each with a neatly folded blanket on top. There were old lace curtains at the windows, no toys, no chest of drawers, no sunshine. Miserable half broken down bathrooms completed the picture. In a word, the place was dismal.

Ah, the children, the children. There was not much hope in their eyes. Their smiles indicated it was good to see us, but they were guarded. They had seen too many disappointments in their lives. The same rather short haircut topped both boys and girls—lice ,you know. Their clothing which was too big, consisted of T-shirts, shorts, pants. They were barefooted. One little girl wore a bright red wool dress, sweating in the July heat.

A teenager in our group had brought a large black suitcase full of small toys from home. I suggested we bring the suitcase to the orphanage and give the children the toys. There seemed to be some problem. It was suggested we give the toys to the matron and she would dole them out, for birthdays, I guess. But I wasn't sure. I had heard that the owners often kept the toys themselves. We decided to distribute the toys ourselves.

When we arrived at the orphanage only about 25 children were there. The head mistress was gone, and the children crowded around us, hoping, knowing that something was inside the suitcase for them. Their excitement mounted.

I told the two young women in charge that we were going to give out the toys. We went inside and decided to lay the toys all out on several of the beds, and then have the kids come in one at a time and pick one toy each.

I prayed a quick prayer about this. We wanted to make sure the children got the toys. The children lined up, little ones first, and waited dutifully outside the closed door.

Inside, we opened the suitcase and our shocked eyes saw that it was the wrong suitcase! The open suitcase was half full of used clothing, and those were mostly adult size. Yes, it contained some toys, but not nearly enough for everyone. What should we do? I prayed desperately, and the answer that popped into my head was, "Give out what you have." So we proceeded.

The little children's faces shone when they came in one by one to choose a toy. The mood was one of ecstasy, pure ecstasy. One little girl let out a delighted squeal as she found and hugged a light blue plush pony. I have never seen children so thrilled as these.

But the toys were going fast and to our dismay about twenty more children appeared. They had been out in the woods or down at the river swimming when we arrived and must have got word of the treasure.

There were colored glass beads and skeins of yarn so I suggested we cut yard strands and give out beads for bracelets to the older girls.

In the meantime the older kids had barged in. I was directing the disappointed boys to the clothing, which some didn't want. My teenaged helper wasn't able to control the giving out of the beads, and girls grabbed handfuls of them and stuffed them in their pockets, leaving some girls with nothing. About a dozen children waiting outside the door had to be told that the gifts were all gone.

My heart ached. I went outside the building and noticed a bunch of boys milling around looking disgruntled. They were about twelve to fourteen years old, although it was hard to tell because they were small for their ages. One boy sat on a bench looking sad. I went over to him and asked, "Did you get anything?"

He must have understood English because he answered, "No." What could I give him, dear God! I had on a shiny metal wire bracelet, picked up at a yard sale for 50 cents. I took it off and offered it to him. "Would you like this, it's all I have."

He gave me a smile and took the bracelet and began to turn it around looking at it. Other boys came over to see it.

When we got back to the hotel I went into my room and burst into tears. "Life is so unfair," I cried to my room mate, "and I just made it more unfair." Why, God, oh why wasn't there enough to go around?

Like the loaves and the fishes, would the kids share their toys? It was all I could hope for. Did I make a terrible mistake? Maybe I should have just given the suitcase to the people in charge, like it was suggested. But then I remembered that I had prayed and had acted on my answer. When you're doing God's will, shouldn't everything turn out roses?

I asked the missionaries to please take the other suitcase out to that orphanage and make sure that the children that didn't receive anything the first time, receive a gift. I don't know if they did.

When we arrived home we gave a presentation to our church on a Sunday morning. We asked for help for the orphanage and the people gave generously. They even voted to support the orphanage as part of the church's mission pledge.

I cannot second-guess God. I know that His thoughts are higher than my thoughts and his timing is perfect. I can only trust that that gift giving at the orphanage, however short it seemed to fall, was not a mistake.

"Trust in the Lord with all your heart and lean not on your own understanding...."
(*Proverbs 3: 5*)

The Land

I had long since gotten used to the idea of giving up my house. As a pastor transferring to another town, we'd be selling the home we'd lived in for 27 years. We had raised our children there and worked there. We had roots in that place. But I had known this would happen. The children had grown up and gone and my husband had retired from his teaching job. Our plan was to move when I received my next pastoral assignment. We were selling our house and moving away.

I could give up the house. I'd been weaning myself away from it for quite some time. But when the house was sold the land would go with it. It was a painful realization.

Driving across the countryside to visit our new location, my vision took in the rural scene – small farms, country homes, fields and fields of ripening corn and grain. Hills rising to make a background in all directions. Suddenly the thought struck me. I wasn't going to have any land, not any land of my own.

My grandpa had been a farmer. The reclaimed forest he worked had been transformed from forest into rich black soil, the muck land. As children we used to go down to the muck land and view the acres of celery or potatoes growing there. Grandpa had a small garden of his own there too, and he defied us to find a single weed.

Oh, that land was nice! The buzz of bees was the only sound we heard as we turned our sun-lit faces to look down the rows. What a pleasant place. Grandpa's pride in the land drew me in! I learned that it was good to have land.

The home I was leaving had a big back yard that stretched out past what had once been the garden, across a large, fenced-in pasture for the neighbor's horses, and down to a creek that twisted and meandered along. How often I had taken my little children down to play at the creek. I would sit and think while they waded or uncovered stones looking for crayfish. Beyond the creek rose a big hill displaying the beauties of whatever season was upon it.

Even though we didn't own all this land it was part of "my land"; my daily view from my window, my extension of my backyard.

The parsonage into which we were moving had only a tiny backyard which backed upon another house.

As I was commuting to my new pastorate for a few months until the parsonage was available, I talked to God about the situation. Driving along the verdant hills, laced by ponds and streams, my heart rose up to the Lord,

"I don't have any land," I groaned. Ashamed as I was to lament my loss, because it was a small sacrifice compared to what many people made to the Lord, still, it was my honest feeling. God knew it anyway, so why try to hide it.

The sun lit up the red and orange and golden leaves on the trees as fall erased summer. Clumps of darkest green evergreens nestled among the colors making a perfect contrast. As I drove along soaking in this beauty, I remembered that God "owns the cattle on a thousand hills." Not only that, He owns the hills themselves. As I pondered this it seemed as if the Lord said to my heart, "I own all this, what land would you like?"

I began to smile. I knew exactly what land I wanted. I had already visited it and walked the two miles around the little lake located just seven miles from where we were to live. "Allegany State Park and Red House Lake, that's what I'll take," was my response.

"It's yours," came back the answer to my heart. Suddenly the anxiety of being landless lifted. I began to laugh at this enlightenment. The bigger view of all I owned filled me with delight. I even related this realization to my new parishioners, closing my remarks with a smile. "So, now you know who owns Allegany State Park," I said. "I do."

"See, I have given you this land." (Deuteronomy 1: 8)

A Dutiful Daughter

It was with great anticipation that we were to host a Japanese exchange student, Megumi, for the year. My husband, Ron, and I envisioned a time of sharing cultures, helping our student learn English, and learning a little Japanese from her.

We had plans to show her our nearby attractions: Letchworth Park with its beautiful falls and gorge, and of course Niagara Falls. We hoped to visit Washington, D.C., and then take her to California when we flew there to visit our youngest daughter and her husband. Perhaps we would take her to see New York City, too.

How thrilled we were to bring home this beautiful Japanese girl. What mystery surrounded those dark eyes and shy ways! She arrived in August and those last two weeks of summer gave us a chance to get acquainted. All went well.

Then, for Megumi, disaster struck. When school started, Megumi found that her ability to speak and understand English fell far short of the minimum requirement for the senior class courses she was taking. School was impossibly hard. Depression followed.

On the weekends, she lay in her bed and did not want to get up. After painstaking tries on our part to communicate with her, she would only say, "Sick, sick," and point to her head or stomach. Then she would turn her face to the wall and those dark eyes would shut, closing out the world. She was too sick to go to church or to go to visit relatives for family activities. We knew that she was undoubtedly homesick and this was to be expected. But after several weekends and several missed school days because of stomach pain I decided to take her to the doctor.

The doctor kindly took time to try to communicate with Megumi via the spoken word and also by using her electronic dictionary. He checked her over physically and took blood tests. After finding out about her struggles with the class work he deduced that her illness was probably due to stress. It was real pain indeed, but caused by stress.

What to do? The doctor's eyes met mine over her head and he said, "Perhaps this is too much for her." He urged Megumi to concentrate on learning English and not worry so much about the other subjects. She nodded agreement but came home still crouched over in pain.

God answers prayer. That's all there is to it. We found out that there was a Japanese pastor in a town 25 miles away. On the phone he very well understood the predicament and volunteered to come over the next day for a visit. He showed up with his wife and two babies.

The minute Pastor Chiba opened his mouth and spoke in Japanese to her, Megumi's face lit up like a Christmas tree. She sat up straight, no longer clutching her stomach. Her animated voice lilted through the house. I was amazed, literally amazed. With my permission, the Chibas invited her to travel to Rochester to pick up some Japanese food at an oriental food store.

The door closed with a flurry of laughter and activity. I sat down on the couch alone and wept tears of relief. The pressure was off. God had provided help. I was also getting an insight into just how insidious psychosomatic illness can be.

We hired a tutor to help Megumi with the English language. The teacher was a remedial reading teacher at the grade school and of oriental background herself. Our hope was that Megumi would become more comfortable with speaking English. She enjoyed the teacher's company and looked forward to the weekly sessions.

A pattern was emerging for Megumi's life here. She walked home from school with the girl next door. Upon entering the house, she went straight upstairs to her room and closed the door. She slept until supper when we called her downstairs. If I asked, she would help set the table and get supper on. She liked all our food and so eating was pleasant even if conversation lagged.

Ron and I would try simple, relaxed conversation which somehow always deteriorated into something resembling a grilling session. "How was school today?" She shrugged her shoulders. "What's your favorite class."

Silence, then the answer, "Gym." Ron tried kidding with her. That fell flat, even after she became more proficient with the language. Hard as we tried to communicate, it was a one way street. She simply answered our questions with one or two words.

After supper she helped clear away the dishes, then scooted back up to her room. There she would stay until we went up to bed. Then she would come downstairs, get on the computer and e-mail her friends in Japan. After that she would study until 2 or 3am. Basically Ron and I felt hurt and rejected. Our cheerful, "good morning" met only with a quiet "eh" sound. How to communicate?

We invited the church youth group over for a party. We arranged some meetings with neighbor girls. Megumi appeared to enjoy these times but nothing came of it. Early on we found out that she did not like American school or American students but we hoped over time that would change. However, she was an avid student and worked night and day at her school work. She managed to be on the Honor Roll at school the entire year. We praised her.

Megumi was not interested in going to church. We negotiated with her to attend with us once a month, as church was important to us. On those occasions she stood with us to shake hands with the congregation afterwards and was pleasant with everyone. She seemed to realize what was expected of her as "pastor's daughter."

If Megumi seemed totally preoccupied with her studies on a daily basis, holidays were a different matter. She eagerly took part in the Thanksgiving feast and in the Christmas family festivities. She liked traveling to visit our relatives, touring here and there, and shopping expeditions.

As the school year wore on, there was still no communication other than absolute essentials. Ron helped her many nights on her English book reading assignment, but no small talk would result. Finally we asked her if she would rather spend the second half of the year living with a family that had students at home. (All of our children had grown up and left home. We remembered how different it had been when we had hosted exchange students three times during those years). But Megumi surely understood our question because she answered us in a clear sentence, "No, I am happy here. I want to stay here." We felt relieved. Maybe we were doing a better job than we thought. Probably her expectations were different than ours.

Spring came. We took our exciting trip to California, which Megumi enjoyed. After the trip Megumi tried out for girls' softball at school. She made the team and, even though she didn't play much, she liked being a part of the group. Just as we expected would happen, nearing her time to leave, life eased up for her. She started making a few friends, one an exchange student from Germany.

There was still no heart to heart communication between us, no sharing about real life in Japan, or about big differences between our cultures. We were so eager to find out about her way of thinking and her culture. I wrote in my journal: "May 30. All these months—and I don't have a glimpse of who she really is. Lord, help us in these last weeks to "get through to her."

Then the thought came to me: Megumi's aim here in our house is to be a dutiful daughter. She is not interested in us per se, but wishes to do what is pleasing. That is her focus rather than sharing her life or being close friends with us. I looked at the positive side. She shows us respect, is neat and clean, keeps her room neat, helps with dishes, stays at the table until everyone is done, is a conscientious student, goes to church once a month and is pleasant to everyone, and doesn't give us any trouble.

A revelation hit me—God was teaching me through Megumi about my life with the Lord. I could now understand how hurt and frustrated he must feel, when he receives only my meager attention, without life, without spirit, only asking *please* for what I need, or want.

I thought, "Now Lord, I understand how you, Jesus, feel about us. You want us to be more than just dutiful servants. You want our love and sharing. Forgive me when I have not been interested in communicating with you. For many years, I only gave you a relationship at a distance, programmed to meet my need."

Now I truly understand what Jesus meant when he said to his disciples, *"I no longer call you servants....Instead, I have called you friends." (John 15: 15)*

Beautiful, dutiful Japanese daughter, perhaps some day you will understand and return to be our close and dearly loved friend.

The Face of Grief

The face of grief
looks far away
with eyes that stare
and avoid your look.
Grief is so very personal
a wanting to hide
and yet, a need to be held close,
understood, in silence.

The wail of pain
echoes across the ages
A mournful sound
rising from deep inside
An animal cry
for one who is gone
never to return
The loss is great, beyond words

Then comes numbness
and robot actions;
the feet move, the mouth speaks,
the hand picks up the fork to eat.
Rote movements, signifying
that life goes on
Deep sighs, memories, tears
The pain of life.

The face of grief
I recognize that face
For it has been my own.

And They Lived Happily Ever After

That's what the fairy tales say of the hero and heroine, "and they lived happily ever after." And that's what many people believe is the goal in life. The "good life" we see as "health, wealth, and happiness" or some semblance of it, and, of course, we thank God for it when we have it.

But is that God's main goal, His main plan for us? No. God wants far, far more for us than that. Jesus said, "I have come that they might have life, and have it more abundantly" (KJV) or "to the fullest" (NIV) John 10:10. The word that is used for "life" here is *zoe*, meaning spiritual life, not *bios*, meaning physical life. The abundant life then, or the life of fullness that Jesus came to give us, is the spiritual life. And how are we most likely to grow in the spiritual life? The answer is usually through sacrifice, suffering, concern for others, and obedience to God's commands.

That doesn't sound like the current American thought of the good life, which would avoid all or most of those things. Yet as we look at the people that we see as the most worthwhile or helpful people, we usually see someone who has suffered through blasted hopes, disappointments, set backs and sorrows, and has come out on top—

an overcomer, someone who still has the joy of the Lord, despite all things. That person can help us along the way. That person has attributes of great value.

In light of that, let us focus on living for God, according to the pattern of Christ. Let's not strive for the world's idea of the good life, but rather strive to be in tune with God's plan for our life. Those qualities we develop in becoming an overcomer on this earth, are ours forever. In this way we will indeed live "happily ever after" in His love here. And in eternity.

"Do not conform any longer to the pattern of this world, but be transformed by the renewing of your mind. Then you will be able to test and approve what God's will is—his good, pleasing and perfect will." (Romans 12:2)

Gerbil

Overgrown mouse, glorified rat
                    how come
                              you get such a place of honor
                                        in my home?
glassed-in cage
        sawdust floor
            fancy tissue bed
                wild bird seed, yet at 2.50 a bag
exercise wheel
            complete with adoring audience to watch you
                                        perform
                                        delight in your every move
            Some other time
                or place
                    you would have been
                            The scourge of the house and even
                                        the nation.
Caught in traps
    hunted by cats

gotten rid of by any means possible
                                a pestilence.
What folly or fad
                dictates your life
                        and my acceptance of you?
                                never earning love or hatred
                                        by your own merit,
Worthy only if public opinion
                        decrees it so.
I leave you in your fancy cage.

Ready for School

Wipe your nose
don't you have a tissue?
here
Stop sucking your thumb
big girls don't suck their thumbs
Here's your lunch pail
hurry up, the bus is coming
Your sweater's buttoned up wrong
no
start at the bottom and button towards the top
You dropped your milk pennies?
they rolled under the couch?
Oh, for crying out loud
hurry up and find them or you'll be late
Didn't I tell you to take that thumb
out of your mouth?
Remember, ride home on bus 40
the bus is out there.
Hurry up
Bye!
Oh yeah, have a good time.

Decision

Life isn't easy for him. He lies in the hospital bed with a belligerent look on his face. His voice strikes out in anger and despair. "Well, what I'd like to know is, can I play sports? I mean, why should I bother shooting baskets all the time if I can't play basketball? I may as well quit jogging with Dad if I'm not going to be able to go out for track."

I mention that the doctors don't think it's a good idea. I quote some of the things they've said against his playing sports. Living with hemophilia creates some restrictions. I remind him of all the joint bleeds he had in his ankles last spring when he was running. He isn't buying my answers. He doesn't want to hear it. His eyes have a deep hurt and he stares past my head out the window.

What can I say to him, God, what can I say? Do I remind him that there are other things in life? Do I tell him that once you get out of high school, sports aren't so important and you'll want your joints intact? Do I ask him if it's worth the price? What can I say, God, that would make him feel any better? My perspective is not his. My view of life is not his. What can I say to a fifteen year old boy who learned how to play ping-pong left handed when his right elbow became damaged? Who spent hours and days practicing and went on to win the high school championship, county championship, and bi-county championship. To a boy whose buddies all play sports, whose older brothers play sports, whose father is a coach.

Todd, Todd, it is so hard, that your dreams and hopes along this line will have to fade, that the glamour and the excitement of competitive sports can never be yours. It hurts. It hurts worse than the pain of the hemorrhaging. It hurts worse than the two months on crutches now facing you. Your eyes tell how much it hurts.

I can't say anything more. There is nothing that will help right now. My chatter won't change the situation. It is something you must endure. I let the moment pass.

I look around the room and down at my hands. Todd is still staring out the window.

Please God, open another door for him.

"For men are not cast off by the Lord forever. Though he brings grief, he will show compassion, so great is his unfailing love. For he does not willingly bring affliction or grief to the children of men." (Lamentations 3:31-33)

And, in time, God did. Todd became fascinated with electronics, which gave him a step into a career in Computer Science. Perhaps it was his trials that now give him, as a manager, a special understanding and compassion in working with the employees under him.

How Are We Programming our Children?

One of the Christmas cards we received from out-of-town acquaintances was a nicely done computer print-out with words of Christmas greetings, pictures of their family, and an enclosed two page print-out with a Senior picture of their lovely daughter. On her pages were neatly listed 39 achievements of her high school career thus far, in the categories of Academics, Student Government, Interscholastic Athletics, Music, Community service, and other extra-curricular activities. An impressive array, and one that her parents were proud of, I'm sure.

But when I read it, I cringed. This girl was programmed for success—career success, worldly success. She was probably going on to a fine college. Yet something was missing. There was nothing about church or God or religious affiliation. And how will probable marriage and children fit in with this training?

Thinking back to my own high school career, I realized there was very little in all those achievements of mine that prepared me for marriage and staying home with children. Those two worlds were as different as they could be.

When our children came along, I chose to stay home with them, and dearly loved raising them, but it wasn't at all what I was programmed for. I often felt like life was passing me by. Only years later did I realize that mothering was the most important work I could do.

Programming our children to be career-oriented first and foremost can set them up for dissatisfaction with the "nuts and bolts" of the everyday life of marriage and children. And what about God? God sets our relationships with Himself and with other people at the highest level. His greatest commandment is to love Him, "with all our heart, soul, mind, and strength, and second to it, love our neighbor as ourself." (Mark 12:30, 31) Do our priorities and our actions and what we praise our children for, show this to be true, or do we jump on the secular bandwagon and put worldly achievements first?

To "gain the whole world, and lose our own soul" would be a terrible waste of a human life, and yet isn't that what the world programs us for? Even as Christians we come under the same sort of worldly programming because we are affected by the society around us.

So, what is the answer? Christian parents need to "talk the talk," and "walk the walk," in order to combat the world view shown to their children. Parents need to constantly point out the false message it teaches. We need to praise and prioritize the necessity and the rewards of Christian living, especially in marriage and child raising. It sounds like a big job and it is! But the alternative is to let the world woo our children away.

The apostle Paul lists all his inheritances and achievements as a very successful Hebrew Pharisee (see Phil. 3:5,6), and then he turns around and tosses them all away, calling them rubbish. They mean nothing to him anymore, next to knowing Christ. (see Phil. 3:7, 8) Paul's viewpoint is my prayer for the lovely girl on the Christmas letter, as well as for all our church family students.

Let's not let our children, nor ourselves, get sucked into the world view of success.

"Bring up your children in the training and instruction of the Lord." (Ephesians 6:4)

The YoYo Effect

When I first became a pastor of a little country church in the summer of 1984, my spirits were up. It was so exciting and thrilling working for the Lord in this way.

The church and Sunday School were full, and going great. I just knew we were impacting that neighborhood for the Lord, and not only the neighborhood, but also people were coming from miles around.

Then September came. The Sunday morning after Labor Day, I stepped into the pulpit and looked out at the congregation to find that over one quarter of the people were missing.

In shock, I inquired of a group of the faithful, "Where did everybody go?" "Oh," came back the casual reply, "Church softball season is over and many of the players only come to church to play softball." (In the church softball league, Sunday morning attendance was a prerequisite to play during the week). My spirits fell. I was struck with the reality that those enthusiastic young men, some with wives and children, were not committed to the Lord, but to the game.

That was my first encounter with the spiritual yo-yo effect: spirits "up" one week or month, spirits "down" the next, depending on the enthusiasm of the body or the rate of attendance, or both.

Sunday School teachers, and youth group leaders and Bible study leaders face the same experience. One week ten smiling-faced kids or adults, next week one or two, or even none. Especially in a small church or group even one person makes a difference. Church leaders know that success is not dependant on numbers, but when a Sunday School teacher spends hours preparing the lesson only to find that no one shows up that Sunday, it is a real "downer" (there goes the yo-yo effect again).

True, some Sundays there will be an avalanche of illness or a holiday when many are away visiting relatives, or a job that forces one to work on Sunday, but for some it is simply a lack of commitment. Church does not seem really important; merely one option among many for Sunday morning. Keeping the Sabbath day holy hasn't been learned or retained or put into practice. Sunday morning enticements are many in our society and lure the uncommitted into their promise of entertainment.

Over the years I learned to roll with the punches. I found that the yo-yo that went down would usually roll back up. But often it took time. Most of those young men in my first church did eventually come into the church to stay. I still remember one of them saying to me that he and his wife and children decided to attend every Sunday because their marriage went better when they went to church. Praise the Lord!

It seems that Jesus even struggled with the yo-yo effect. After preaching an unpopular sermon on his body and blood (John 6:53-69), many of his disciples turned back and no longer followed him. Jesus turned to the twelve for assurance. "You do not want to leave me too, do you?" Jesus asked the twelve. Simon Peter answered him, "Lord, to whom shall we go? You have the words of eternal life."

Thank goodness for the faithful ones in the church, who keep the yo-yo on an upward swing. They are the mainstay of the church and Christ will reward their faithfulness on His return.

"Who then is the faithful and wise manager whom the master puts in charge…it will be good for that servant whom the master finds doing so (faithful) when He returns."
(Luke 12: 42,43)

A Change of Opinion

I must admit it. When I first saw the house on the corner of Broad and Academy Streets being painted, I was aghast. Why would anyone paint their house pink and bright blue, and yellow and scarlet? I thought, yuk! Ugh! Horrible! (Sorry, owners).

But then, as I drove by the house every day, I began to look at it differently. A new porch was being put on. I began to be interested in the house. What had been a conventional, old-fashioned house was being changed into something different. I still wasn't sure of the colors, but it didn't look so bad to me.

Then came the day when I began to look for the house as I drove by, thinking "Neat," "Unique," "Different," "Hey, I like it!" Someone is expressing their individuality. The house looked lively. This is a house to point out to visiting relatives.

My total turn around of opinion on the house made me pause and realize what a product we are of learning preference for the familiar, and therefore prone to prejudice for the unfamiliar. Somehow we get programmed into the tyranny of the familiar. Perhaps that's where racism and bigotry and Phariseeism come from. "They're different. Their taste is different from mine. Therefore, there must be something wrong."

Suspicion sets in. Then rejection. Then hostility. How foolish we are. And all the while the Creator in heaven, who made no two snowflakes alike, looks down and shakes His head and says, "*Who created all these?*" Wake up and enjoy my beautiful world and all its diversity.

What about Halloween?

Next to Christmas, my kids always liked Halloween best. About a week before the "big day," we'd scurry around making up costumes or rigging up something like lights on a hat that lit up by connection to a battery. It all seemed like fun; a chance to dress up as a favorite character, be it ballerina or gorilla.

The scary symbolism of Halloween escaped us. Witches, goblins, and ghosts seemed like made-up stuff meant to scare people. "Tricks or treats" was the big focus, and with eight kids, we ate the candy horde for days.

Then, somewhere along the line, my consciousness was raised. There really were witches and warlocks out there, and satanic cults perpetrating all kinds of evil. And their big "celebration of evil" night was—you guessed it—Halloween. It made me uncomfortable.

Still, when I pastored my first church, it didn't bother me that they put on a big Halloween party every year at the church for kids and adults. Even people that never attended church would show up in costume to bob for apples, enjoy the cider and donuts, and race around the fellowship hall playing games.

Then, one Halloween night when we arrived at the church, I opened the door to the fellowship hall. The room was dimly lit and the decorating committee had covered the walls with witches, skeletons and ghosts. A little child was screaming in terror over a life-sized Herman Munster tacked on the wall glaring at him.

It hit me like a ton of bricks. This symbolism is all of death and of evil. There is no place for it in the Christian church. Christ stands for life, and beauty and joy and freedom.

After that I told my church board my strong feelings and we ruled out any more church Halloween parties. We tried to replace it by dressing up as Pilgrims and Indians for the Thanksgiving dinner. Christians through the centuries have dealt with pagan holidays by Christianizing them; making them fit the Christian culture. Perhaps celebrating on a different day, calling it a Harvest party or Biblical Character Costume event will fill the bill.

As Christians, we need to always take stock of what we're doing and what we're teaching our children. In no way should we aid and abet the enemy. We cannot serve both good and evil. The Bible says, *"Have nothing to do with the fruitless deeds of darkness." (Ephesians 5:11)* Take a second look at Halloween.

Keep Your Mind
on Higher Things

No, I did not read the Starr report transcript on the internet. I particularly wished to avoid all the explicit details of President Clinton's sexual encounters with a young woman, not his wife. That his deeds be exposed may be necessary, but that it be done so graphically and in detail is inappropriate and destructive. The word of the Lord says, "Have nothing to do with the fruitless deeds of darkness, but rather expose them, for it is shameful even to mention what the disobedient do in secret." (Ephesians 5:11,12)

The Starr report contains much "shameful" stuff. Why the Congress wanted it all made public, down to the last detail, I'm not sure. (Couldn't they have modified it to put "delete, delete" in the places that are shameful to mention.) There is a need to expose the matter (surely your sins will find you out!), but then isn't it just as shameful to talk about it, dwell upon it, become saturated with it? Unfortunately, that's exactly what the media does. And we participate in it by listening. It constantly advertises the works of sin. Clinton's act of adultery doesn't have to be explicitly spelled out. We get the picture.

Along with many others, I'm concerned about the impact this whole mess has had upon our young people. Now they have seen and heard, in detail, the whole sordid sin (yes, let's call sin, sin). This has been devastating to the moral fiber of impressionable young people. They think, if our president is doing it, so can we.

It has made it easier for them to follow their baser nature. It has further eroded, if not totally destroyed, any high ideals they had about the decency of the president, and consequently of government in general. Parents are going to find it tougher yet to instill strong moral values, and honor for the government and the laws of the land, in their children.

The only thing that uplifts people is to get our minds upon higher things; thoughts that are uplifting. *"Whatever is right, whatever is pure, whatever is lovely, whatever is admirable—if anything is excellent or praiseworthy —think about such things." (Philippians 4:8)* This does not mean to bury our heads in the sand over current events, but it does mean to choose not to dwell upon them, and seek higher thoughts.

I look all around me at good people who do decent things, people that seek to be like Christ, people who desire things of high value and moral soundness for their children. Let's get up out of the muck and mire. Let's get some decent people in high office. Let's enforce some stringent decency codes on the media in all areas, including entertainment. I'm sick of this mess. I think most of the American people are, too.

God is Not My Water-Boy

God is not my water-boy
Here to serve my every prayer
Get me this, take me there
Remove each stone and barrier

Rescue me, surely He will
Save me from all harm
For in my little world
I'd be free from all alarm

But what about the world outside
That moans and groans and fears
Lord, must I receive a dreaded answer
So that others may endure?

If this is so, then I must see
And look beyond my plan
If some would gain through my loss or pain
Then I put it in God's hand

God is not my water-boy
Rather, his servant must I be
A willing one, a joyful one
Whatever His answer to me.

On Handling Conflict

I don't like being in conflict with anybody, or having to handle conflict. I don't think that most people do. At least not many. And yet if we're living we've got it. We run into it. Relationships aren't without conflict.

How to handle it. Avoid it like the plague? Turn your back and walk away? Complain to everybody else? Shout the other person down?

The Bible has answers if we remember to look there and follow the directions. In Matt. 18:15-16 Jesus says, "If your brother sins against you, go and show him his fault, just between the two of you. If he listens to you, you have won your brother over. But if he will not listen, take one or two others along, so that every matter may be established by the testimony of two or three witnesses."

No avoidance tactics here. Basically, confront the other person. In order to get things out in the open. In order to get things worked out. In order for there to be peace between you.

But confronting other people isn't easy. It's a good way of getting your head knocked off, or at least your ears burned, and having to learn that other painful "Jesus lesson" of turning the other check.

I've not yet found the perfect way to confront, or even an acceptable way. If you're too vague the other person doesn't "get it." If you're too strong or too graphic the other person gets hurt, angry, retaliates or gives you the cold shoulder for a good long time. If it's church member they may walk out and not return. Yet if you're in a leadership position, be it family, work, social or civic organizations, one of our jobs is, at times, to confront and correct.

Nobody likes to hear about their short-comings or wrong doings (me, either). So no matter how you sugar coat that pill, it's a hard one to swallow.

The trick of learning to confront is to do it without anger, contempt, or condemnation. That takes a good bit of practice and maturity.

It is said that Saint Dominic, who lived in the 13th century, beautifully illustrated the tender way of Jesus. "He reprimanded others justly and so affectionately that no one was ever upset by his correction and punishment, even though the penances were sometimes very severe." (The Divine Conspiracy by Dallas Willard). No wonder he was deemed a Saint! There's one man that should have been cloned. We could hire him out to do the dirty work for the rest of us.

But short of that, we still have to handle conflict on our own. My prayer is, "Teach me, Lord, how to handle it in your way." I'm afraid I'll be in this school of learning for a long time.

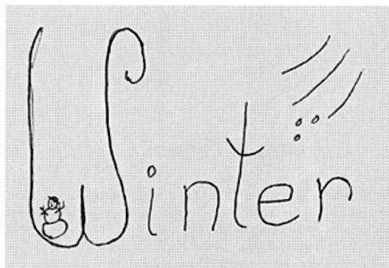

"If I rise on the wings
of the dawn --- your hand
will guide me"

(Psalm 139: 9, 10)

Christmas Coming Again

Christmas seems to be a time of extremes. On the one side there is the time of hilarity, so to speak. There are parties with special food and desserts—yum! There are friends and family get-togethers with talk and laughter and playing games. There's watching family videos playing back the year's events. The camera flashes as we take our "Christmas this year" pictures.

Then there's the trimming of the tree—the decorations—the lights—the candles. Oh—there's Jingle Bells and Frosty the Snowman and How the Grinch Stole Christmas.

And, oh yes, picking just the right Christmas cards to send, and just the right gifts for everyone on your list. A busy time, a fun time; one we wouldn't miss for anything! The hoopla and the hilarity of Christmas.

But then there's the other side of Christmas, the other extreme. If one side is hilarity and hoopla the other side is quietness and thoughtfulness. It's letting our soul absorb the deepness of life. It's a walk out doors at night in the softly falling snow. It's looking up at the stars and asking God what life's really all about. And listening for an answer. It's the babe in the manger. It's Silent Night, and Hark! The Herald Angels Sing.

It's carols sung in the nursing home and food baskets to the needy and quarters dropped into the Salvation Army bucket. It's memories of other Christmases, and hopes, and yes, tears. It's a settling of the soul into the arms of God, and knowing, somehow, that life has meaning because Christ was born. As we enter the Christmas season, may your days contain some of both extremes, but especially the latter.

Living with Change

Did you ever notice that the Lord doesn't let his beloved people get too comfortable, too complacent? No sooner do we get ourselves comfortably settled than the Lord pulls the rug out from under us, so to speak. Look at some of our biblical characters. Young David was a contented shepherd boy—until God led him to fight the giant. Jonah was comfortable as a prophet until the Nineveh assignment. Esther was a settled queen until she was forced to take risky action for the sake of her people's destiny. Mary's young womanhood was abruptly and forever interrupted by the announcement from the angel Gabriel. The big fisherman, Peter, had his daily life changed when he was swept into discipleship with Christ.

The path of least resistance is a rut. How we love our ruts. They are well-worn and comfortable. But they don't change us. They don't change the status quo. They don't change the world. We sing, "From Glory To Glory, He's changing Me," but do we really want those uncomfortable or even painful changes?

I believe that God either allows or causes changes in order for us to move on in our spiritual growth. The more we resist or fight the change the more we struggle against God. The quicker we yield and see the change as coming from the hand of God, the quicker we accomplish what God desires, both in our lives and in the world. God wants us to be champions, not loafers. Consider each change that comes into your life, whether wanted or unwanted, as an opportunity coming from God. Agree to fight the giant, take the assignment, get out of the boat. And see what God can do!

"You have stayed long enough on this mountain....Go in and take possession of the land...." (Deuteronomy 1:6,8)

Fear Not, for I Am with You

*Are not two sparrows sold for a penny? Yet not one of them will
fall to the ground apart from the will of your Father. And even
the very hairs of your head are all numbered. So don't be afraid;
you are worth more than many sparrows. (Matthew 10: 29-31)*

There is a Peanuts cartoon by Charles Schultz entitled "Trapped
by an Icicle!" It's a winter day and Snoopy is in his doghouse with
snow on the roof. His doghouse is backed up against the side of the
family house, and there is a huge icicle hanging off the house roof,
right above the door of his doghouse. Snoopy is inside his doghouse
with his nose sticking out, thinking, *It's silly to be trapped in a
doghouse by an icicle.* In the next picture Snoopy thinks, *I think I'll
just make a run for it! I think I'll just zoom out of here!* In the third
vignette Snoopy is still lying in his doghouse thinking, *I think I'll just
leap up and zoom right out!* Alas, the last picture gives us Snoopy's
thought, *I think I'll just lie here for the rest of my life!* Trapped by an
icicle! Trapped by fear it will fall and hit him.

Just like Snoopy, we humans are plagued by fear. There's
claustrophobia—fear of a confined space or closed room,

hydrophobia—fear of water. Agoraphobia—fear of being in open spaces or crossing open spaces. Besides these, we have to deal with the more common fears of failure, fear of being alone, fear of loss, fear of poor health, fear of old age, fear of what other people think of us, fear of injury, fear of falling. Still others are afraid of not being attractive to the opposite sex, of not pleasing God, or parents, fear of driving in city traffic, fear of dryness, of lack of creativity, or of baseball batting average. We worry about being attacked by the devil, animals, burglars or the school bully, and the list goes on.

Psychologists tell us that human beings' two greatest fears are: death or what leads to death and secondly, fear of public speaking.

Is it any wonder, then, that Jesus comes to us, (and the prophets before him) saying, "Do not be afraid of them, for I am with you, and will rescue you. " (Jeremiah 1:8) God does not want human beings in bondage to fear.

Fear does not come from God.

Fear is one of Satan's great weapons against us. If he can fill us with fear:

We will never speak out against an injustice.

We will never share our faith.

We will never take a risk for Jesus or go on a dangerous mission.

We will never go out for a sport or a drama team.

We will never get out of our comfort zone, or make changes in our life.

We will never preach, teach, do Jr. church, sing, shout for joy, or raise our hands in worship, for fear we may make a fool of ourselves, or fail, or be inadequate. Satan will paralyze us with fear, if he can, every bit as much as Snoopy was paralyzed by fear in his doghouse. (By the way, are you in the doghouse, paralyzed by that icicle of fear?) Satan wants to take away our confidence in God, thus bringing us under his power. But the apostle John says, "We know and rely on the love God has for us. God is love…. There is no fear in love. But perfect love drives out fear." (I John 4: 16, 18)

My husband and I lost our nine month old daughter, Robin, after an accident. It left us devastated. Many years went by and we had other children. Often I was plunged into a great fear that we could lose another child. Kids do all kinds of stuff. I would see the older children ride off on their bikes down the road, and a semi truck would come rolling along, and I'd be clutched by fear. "What if my son's bike hit a stone and he fell into the path of the semi?" In fear I cried out to the Lord, "Let anything happen to me but please, please don't let anything happen to another child. I couldn't bear it!" I bargained: my life for theirs, but that didn't take away the fear.

Finally one day I turned around and faced the fear that had dogged me for many years. I stood and said, *"Yes, it would be terrible if I lost another child. Yes, I would suffer awful grief. But I could bear it. God would get me through it."* Immediately the fear left. It vanished completely. And I was free. *"Resist the devil, and he will flee from you." (James 4:7)* He has to because Christ has the power.

Jesus encourages us when he speaks of God's overshadowing care, *"The very hairs of your head are all numbered. Are not two sparrows sold for a penny? Yet not one them will fall to the ground apart from the will of your Father. Fear not, you are worth more than many sparrows." (Matt 10:29-31)*

When it is in God's will, He gives divine protection over us.

In II Kings 6:8-23, there is a wonderful story of the prophet Elisha in a tight spot. Israel was at war with Aram. The King of Aram was enraged because the man of God; the prophet Elisha, kept uncovering where his camp was located, and warning Israel's king. As a result the army of Israel was on guard and did not fall into the traps set by Aram.

The king of Aram ordered his officers to find Elisha. They found him in a place called Dothan, so they went by night and surrounded the city with a strong force of horses and chariots. They were going to get this trouble maker, or else! Early the next morning Elisha's servant went out and saw the army of chariots and horses surrounding the city—and he was filled with fear. "Oh my Lord, what shall we do?" the servant cried out.

What did the prophet answer? *"FEAR NOT. Those who are with us are more than those who are with them."* And Elisha prayed, *"Oh*

Lord, open his eyes so he may see!" Then the Lord opened the servant's eyes, and he looked and saw the hills full of horses and chariots of fire all around Elisha. These were the chariots of the heavenly host—divine protection. As the enemy came down toward him, Elisha prayed to the Lord, *"Strike these people with blindness."* So God struck them with blindness, as Elisha had asked and the battle did not take place. FEAR NOT. When it is God's plan to rescue us, it will be so.

Billy Graham tells a story about missionaries in Africa. A native tribe became hostile to the missionaries living there and set out to kill them. The missionaries saw the advancing warriors and were on their knees in the mission house praying. Strangely, as suddenly as they had arrived, the natives turned and fled. The missionaries had no idea why until years later. The chief had become a Christian, and sitting at a meal, talking with him, they asked him why he hadn't attacked them that night. He answered, "Why, your house was surrounded by warriors!" Divine protection.

How much God would have us overcome fear. The 23rd Psalm tells us: *"Yea, though I walk through the valley of the shadow of death, I will fear no evil."* Why? *"For THOU art with me."* In Revelation 1: 17,18, KJV we read that the glorified Jesus says to us, *"Fear not, I am the first and the last—and behold, I am alive forever more."* In other words: Fear not death, nor what leads to death, nor life beyond the grave. Those strong FEAR NOTS give us reasons for encouragement. God is *with* us. He does not tell us that we won't have to go through trials, but He does tell us that He will be with us in trials.

But now, this is what the Lord says, he who created you…he who formed you… *"FEAR NOT, for I have redeemed you: I have summoned you by name; you are mine. When you pass through the waters, I will be with you; and when you pass through the rivers, they will not sweep over you. When you walk through fire, you will not be burned; the flames will not set you ablaze. For I am the Lord your God…"* *(Isaiah 43: 1-3)* Hang onto that, and God will get you through. Face your fear and resist the devil for we have God's overshadowing care watching over us. In this life we have his divine protection in his will, and God's assurance of life beyond the grave. Death is defeated by Christ.

Do we not owe it to our Lord to never be afraid? To be afraid is doubly an injury to Him. First, it means that we forget Him, and forget that He is with us and is all powerful. Secondly, it means that we are not conformed to his will—for since all that happens is either willed by God, or permitted by God—we ought to rejoice in all that happens to us and feel neither anxiety nor fear. Let us then have faith in God that banishes fear. Our Lord is at our side, with us, upholding us. FEAR NOT.

Pray without Ceasing

Did you ever feel anxious about prayer? I don't pray enough. Anxiety. I don't really know how to pray. Anxiety. God doesn't seem to answer my prayers. Anxiety. So I guess prayer just isn't my thing. I'll try singing or Bible reading instead. If this is the case, the devil laughs all the way home —because prayer is the moving force of God's kingdom. Thus it's extremely important that God's people pray.

A way to look at it, is that prayers are like seeds sown. They all have life in them, the potential for life. So they need to be sown. It is good for you to be the sower. God *always* uses them. Prayer is never in vain. But prayers are not always answered when we want them to be.

It is enough for you to be faithful and sow the seeds. God must give the increase, and will, if it is His will. Remember this, and have no anxiety over it. It is enough to sow the seeds. Be happy. The farmer is happy to sow the seeds knowing that he will see the results of some. So it is for us. The results of the rest of the seeds will be seen in the garden of Heaven. You will see them there. Always pray.

"Pray without ceasing." (I Thessalonians 5:17 KJV)

A Modern Version
of the Christmas Story

In those days Caesar Augustus issued a decree that a census should be taken of the entire Roman world. (This was the first census that took place while Quirinius was governor of Syria.) And everyone went to his own town to register.

So Joseph also went up from the town of Nazareth in Galilee to Judea, to Bethlehem the town of David, because he belonged to the house and line of David. He went there to register with Mary, who was expecting a child. While they were there, the time came for the baby to be born, and she gave birth to her firstborn, a son. She wrapped him in cloths and placed him in a manger, because there was no room for them in the inn.

And there were shepherds living out in the fields nearby, keeping watch over their flocks at night. An angel of the Lord appeared to them, and they were terrified. But the angel said to them, "Do not be afraid. I bring you good news of great joy that will be for all the people. Today in the town of David a Savior has been born to you; he is Christ the Lord. This will be a sign to you: You will find a baby wrapped in cloths and lying in a manger."

Suddenly a great company of the heavenly host appeared with the angel, praising God and saying, "Glory to God in the highest, and on earth peace to men on whom his favor rests."

When the angels had left them and gone into heaven, the shepherds said to one another, "Let's go to Bethlehem and see this thing that has happened, which the Lord has told us about."

So they hurried off and found Mary and Joseph, and the baby, who was lying in the manger. When they had seen him, they spread the word concerning what had been told them about this child, and all who heard it were amazed at what the shepherds said to them. But Mary treasured up all these things and pondered them in her heart. The shepherds returned, glorifying and praising God for all the things they had heard and seen, which were just as they had been told.

(Luke 2:1-20)

What would the story of the birth of Jesus look like if it took place in this century in your hometown? In the Biblical story of Christ's birth, some vivid pictures come to our mind. We envision the lowly manger scene, no room at the inn, Mary giving birth to Jesus, wrapping him in swaddling clothes and lying him in a manger.

Today we see Mary and Joe driving down the expressway in an old jalopy, trying to get to Bethlehem, Pennsylvania where they have to register for the census at the county seat of Joe's hometown. The Honorable Caesar Romano, governor of the state has issued a law mandating a head count of his entire state. Everybody has to go to their home county to sign in at the registrar's office, under penalty of law. Since the deadline is only a few days away, scattered people from all over the country are traveling by the thousands to Pennsylvania to meet the requirement. Mary and Joe are among them.

Joe is worried. Mary is pregnant with that "unusual" (to say the least) pregnancy. Her due date is coming up soon and she's been uncomfortable all day on this wearisome journey. They pull off the expressway at dusk. The roads are becoming clogged with the new fallen snow and visibility is getting bad. They're near enough to their destination so this seems like a good place to stop. Maybe they can get a motel room. Joe breathes a silent prayer. When he sees the "No vacancy" sign on the Holiday Inn, Joe cringes. The Quality Inn and the Days Inn are flashing "No vacancy." Every motel on the strip and within sight are full, full to the brim with Pennsylvanians trying to get to their home counties at the last minute.

Joe's heart falls as he heads the jalopy out of town on the less traveled road. He silently prays that they'll find something out here. There's still a lot of traffic. What a hassle. What a mish-mash of people. Even in this less populated area, no place to park, no place to sleep for the late comers. The El Cheapo Inn has a "No vacancy" sign out front but Joe sees Mary biting her lip, so he decides to pull in and see if he can come up with something.

The desk clerk/owner is feeling frenzied, "Oh good grief! We're full up, and here's a pregnant woman—looks full term to me. Well, nature will take its course, but not tonight, I hope." He looks at Mary with pity, then says to Joe, "Well, you can go out back if you want. Maybe you can set up a place to stay in the bus garage. The buses are out. Good grief! This place is a mad house! Oh, there are some bags of old clothes and blankets for the Salvation Army out there. Use'em if you want." Aside, he says to his helper, "Poor kid, hope she finds someone to help her. The hospital's fifty miles away and they're closing the expressway due to the storm."

Mary and Joe go out to the bus garage. The concrete floor is hard, but they find the bags and the blankets and pile them up for a bed.

Joe looks hopeful, "Here's a kerosene heater. I'll light it up." Soon the heat is warming their chilled bones. Mary spots an empty orange crate.

"Let's see, it'll make a baby bed if the baby comes. I think it's getting near time."

A concerned look crosses Joe's face, "Shore wish we had more, Mary, shore wish we had more. Hey, some lady dropped off this baby blanket." He displays a lovely new looking soft blue blanket. "And

Mary, you brought along some baby clothes, just in case. We shoulda tried to make it to a farm, Mary. But too late now. Is that baby comin? Do you think it'll be born tonight?" Even though Mary and Joe trust in God, it's a difficult time.

This is a rural place, off the expressway, out in the middle of nowhere. By now it's long past midnight. And who's up in the wee hours, who else besides Mary and Joe, that is? Why, farmers get up and down to the barn by 4am. Most folks are home snug in their beds at 4am. Unless you work the graveyard shift at Sheetz. But farmers are up and out, seven days a week, getting ready for milking time. Cows are bawling. Stars are still out. Three hours yet until daylight. Let's look in at the farmers.

Hank: "Hey, that's a peculiar lookin' star. Brightest thing I've ever seen. Hey, come look at this! Annie! Get the hired hands out. They need to come look at this.

Wow! A sign from God for sure. I wonder if it means the end of the world. Help me, God! If I'm gonna die, please take me to heaven! O, God I'm sorry for what I done wrong. I hope it's not too late.

Annie, call George and Minnie. They gotta see this!"

Soon George and Minnie and others arrive. They gather together.

"Everybody here? Let's go up on the hill where we can get a better look!" So the little group trudges up the hill. And suddenly, *whoosh,* a great company of the heavenly host appeared with an angel, praising God.

"Whoa!"

The farmers froze—to a man—and their wives who had come out—eyes glued on the angel and the sky full of heavenly beings.

"Whoa!"

In stunned silence they strained to understand what the angel seemed to be saying. Hank exclaimed, "Yes, I heard it. *Today in town, a Savior has been born. You'll find him in a garage!*" The angels were all praising God, saying, "Glory to God in the highest, and on Earth peace, good will to men."

Suddenly the angels left as quickly as they had come. *Whoosh.* They were gone.

"Wow! Let's go into town and see what's happened. George, you read the Bible; didn't God say He was going to send a Savior? Let's go look and see. That's what the angel said." And so they left their cows, waiting to be milked. Some of the group leaped into the old Chevy pickup and the others into a rusted-out Dodge, and drove as fast as they could into town to scout around and see what they could find. George and his wife Minnie were huddled in blankets bumping around in the truck bed praying like mad on their knees that God would show them just where to go and what to do.

And sure enough they turned in at the right place right off. Out in back of the El Cheapo Inn—in the bus barns, there it was. There *he* was. A newborn baby, sleeping in an orange crate, all snuggled in, peaceful and quiet. The most beautiful thing you ever saw.

Nobody appreciates new life like farmers. They're known to bottle feed a newborn calf that might not make it, or a bummer lamb whose mother rejected him. Farmers have a heart for new life. They see God in it every time. They feel that way about their kids, too—real special—but nothing like this. This baby was beyond words.

Hank related, "Knew it the minute I saw him, that he was the one God brought us to. You could just tell. No doubt about it. God breathed somethin' special into him. Ya know, the young mother and the father thought so, too. A Jewish couple, looked like to me. She had dark hair and brown eyes. That young mother had the look on her face—how can I explain it? No it wasn't pride, though I was sure she was proud of her baby. No, it wasn't relief, though I'm sure she was relieved to have it over with. No, it wasn't even joy. I know what it was! Serenity. 'A peace that passes understanding,' like the Bible says. That's what her face showed. She knew it, too, that God's hand, God's fullness, was on her newborn baby. We all stood in awe for the longest time. And then it was time to go home. Cows had to be milked. They'd be bawlin' by now. We didn't want to leave, but the sun was up. Time to go home. Hired men had gone and got other people to see the baby.

I wonder what God's gonna do now. In this baby, I mean. I wonder what God's gonna do now. And we got to see him! How about that! We got to be a part of it all: the angels praising God! The new born son of God! We got to see it! Just us! Dumb ol' sod-busters! Manure spreaders! Ain't got no status in this town except for hard work. Every nickel I own is tied up in farm machinery. And the bank owns the farm. No education to speak of. Just hard workers. And he came to us! I can't believe it! He came to us! I could cry. I did cry.

My Annie invited 'em to stay here with us for as long as they need—a few days, I guess. She's fixin' up the spare bedroom. Brought down the baby crib from the attic. The kids are all excited. Gonna make him some presents. Pretty exciting. Wonder what God's gonna do with this one. Wonder what God's gonna do now. Shore was nice of Him to let us common folk in on it all. Shore was nice. Thank ya, God. I'm gonna do my best to be a better man."

Miracle?

It seems to me that God often uses natural things and natural events to help us in dire situations. This runs contrary to our expectation that God will have to send a miracle; something supernatural and unique, entirely "other-worldly," to help us or the situation. In our human thinking, we project how God might do it in a spectacular way. For example, in one of the temptations of Jesus in the wilderness, if Jesus had thrown himself off the temple, like Satan tempted him to, Father God would have spectacularly saved him. We would call that a bonafide miracle. Yet God more often uses the mundane resources at hand.

I remember an incident where I was driving a young mother and her three little children to a "safe home" in a city thirty miles away. Her crazed husband had threatened her with a gun, so she was fearful of staying in town lest he find her. She even turned down the offer of staying with my husband and me.

Blizzard conditions were setting in that night when I pulled the car up onto the expressway to head to our destination. The farther we went the worse it got. It was snowing and blowing so hard that visibility was almost zero. Our only guide to staying on the road was keeping between the snow banks that lined the sides of the road. These were visible when we rolled the windows down to look as I drove the car along at snail's pace.

I was praying out loud, with urgency and trust, "Jesus, help us. Protect these children. What should I do? I can't see to get off the expressway. Be with us, Jesus." Suddenly, up ahead, I could make out some blinking lights. A snowplow had pulled up onto the expressway and was slowly plowing along. "Thank God!" I praised him out loud.

I pulled in behind the snowplow and followed him until he exited, with me right behind him. By then we were close to our destination and the visibility was better. Was it a miracle? It was certainly an answer to prayer. God's timing was perfect. Some would say it was a lucky coincidence, but I know better.

"The Lord Almighty is with us; the God of Jacob is our fortress."
(Psalm 46:11)

Living in the Gap

We live in an imperfect world. What an understatement! We aren't on planet Earth very long before we discern that Murphy's law ("things that can go wrong, will") is in effect.

This seems ever so true when we hit the Christmas rush. Expectations run high. Desires are great. Our biggest holiday is coming. We'd like things to be extra nice, not only for ourselves but for other people. And so we buy and plan and work and make and direct and think and call and do.

And we pray that somehow it'll all fit together and be a blessed Christmas. We envision only softly falling snow, angelic children's faces, Christmas carols sung in the lamplight by golden voices, love and harmony, and all those wonderful things that fit the scene. In short, a greater sense of God's presence is the perfection that we hope for.

But in reality we face fatigue, frayed nerves, harsh voices, a kid that doesn't show up to do his part in the Christmas play, squabbling relatives, an elusive "just right" gift we can't find anywhere, hurt feelings, last-minute changes, endless work, a grandchild that throws up all over the living room rug, and worst of all, a sense of missing the sacred peace of the season. In short, we run head on into the imperfect. It hits us with greater impact because our expectations are greater, our desires are loftier and our hopes are higher. We care more. Where is God in all of this?

God decrees that we live out this life in the imperfect. We messed up the perfect at the very beginning. We couldn't take perfection in the Garden of Eden. Adam and Eve got bored and then curious in a perfect environment.

They thought, "Let's try something else." They did and got immediately ushered out of the perfect and into the imperfect. Thorns and thistles now grew in their garden. Life became tough. Murphy's law became a grueling test of human endurance. God allowed it. He even blessed it. Human creatures learn more in the imperfect—about ourselves, that is. We would be perfected only in the struggle. Christmas is a real test. It brings out sharp realization of our shortcomings, and those of others.

The test was there on the first Christmas. Jesus had to live with it too. If we want to find out how to make it through the gap we'd better seek Him out. He managed to walk perfectly in an imperfect world. He bridged the gap. By the time you read this, Christmas may be over and we'll be headed into a new year. Don't worry if you seemingly flunked the Christmas test this year. Consider what you learned. Remember that Jesus' presence comes into the imperfect, always. He'll get us through.

Raymond

Through the open window in my church office I could hear the cursing. The gruff voice belonged to the elderly man who lived down the country road from the church. If his voice was gruff, his manner seemed more so. No warmth exuded from him, at least none that I had detected.

I'd been in his house before. His wife Mary did all the talking. While she chattered away, Raymond read the newspaper. He didn't even look up when I introduced myself. He just gave a grunt and went back to reading his paper.

Mary came to church from time to time. Mostly though, ill health kept her home. The dining room table had rows of pill bottles. Mary was in and out of the hospital repeatedly. They called her a "regular" there. The staff knew her well: the little lady wearing the red flannel pajamas who could tell a good story. They'd pop in on a free moment just to catch the latest.

Raymond seldom came to the hospital to see her. He had trouble walking very far and besides there were things to do at home. A remnant of the once prosperous family farm was there, and Raymond kept busy with a big garden. He'd get on his four wheeler to go the short distance to his garden. Then you'd see him on his hands and knees crawling along the rows to plant or weed or tend the new shoots coming up.

I'd heard stories about Raymond, like what a strong man he'd been in his day, like how he'd moved the old abandoned schoolhouse down to his land to serve as another barn. One time when unloading a bull from a truck, the huge animal had swung around and slammed him up against the side rails. With almost equal force Raymond gave him a mighty shove back.

Yup, he was a legend around the place...but he didn't go to church.

Oh, I'd heard tell that years ago when the church bell was stuck he would climb up on the church roof and up to the steeple to unstick it. In the wintertime he used to stoke the wood stove in the church sanctuary, but he never stayed for the service. Needless to say, everybody was surprised one Sunday afternoon when Raymond showed up for a church dinner. Whispers went all around, "Raymond's here! Brought a dish to pass, too."

Mary's heart got worse and worse. She was home with an oxygen tank to keep her going. The day after Christmas she died. Her teenaged grandson, who slept on the couch in the sitting room where Mary stayed, woke to hear her gasping for breath, but it was too late. Mary was gone.

After that I saw more of Raymond. I made regular visits to his house. We began to talk about farming—my grandpa had been a farmer—and about cooking. The doctor had told old Raymond he'd just better do the cooking when Mary's heart got bad, and no bones about it! Raymond had risen to the challenge and had become an excellent cook.

He questioned me about pie making. I fumbled and fussed and finally admitted that I didn't make pies, except on special occasions, like Thanksgiving. The black eyebrows knit close together and incredulity filled his voice, "Well! You'd think a woman'd be able to make a pie once in a while." Later, when I was at the door, the gruff voice stopped me, "Well, What kind of pie do you like?" After that there was a delicious, freshly made pie ready for me every Sunday. He even bought a special basket for me to carry it in.

I repeatedly invited Raymond to come to church. He answered that he always spent that time cooking dinner for the family members that gathered there to eat every Sunday after the church service.

One Sunday my spirits were down. From the pulpit I could see the gaps where church family members had once sat. Two families of five had moved away. A young couple had married and gone on their way. Several high school grads were now in college. Three members had died and two more were in nursing homes. In this small church it seemed a big loss.

We rose to sing the first hymn. The doors banged open. In came Raymond. The halting steps did not hide the dignity of the old man.

"Oh Lord, you've sent me Raymond!" my heart sang. After that, he came every Sunday and always sat in the same pew, surrounded by his grandchildren and his children.

"Two things I want to get rid of, he said one day. My cursing and this crying all the time. Why, I can't imagine why I cry so much." He'd cried a lot since Mary died.

"I don't know as the crying's so bad Raymond," I answered. It's the people that never cry or can't cry that I feel sorry for."

Raymond had to go to the hospital. I walked down the long corridor and quietly slipped into his room. He was perched on the edge of the bed, reading a Bible, opened to the book of Ruth.

"I didn't know you read the Bible, Raymond, you ought to come to Bible Study.

"Well I wouldn't know enough to ask an intelligent question," he quipped.

When he got home I badgered him. "Let's have Bible Study at your house tonight Raymond.

"Dining room table's a mess. You'd never find a place to sit down."

"I'll help you clean it off. How about it? We'll have it here...is that alright?"

"Well, I guess so," the voice was gruff again.

After that, Bible Study and Prayer Group met at Raymond's most every Wednesday night.

Seasons flew by. Raymond was busy with his garden and canning and pickling and drying apples and numerous other things. Winter came. The phone in my office rang. It was Raymond. "I've got a pot of tea on and I just made fresh cookies. Thought you might want to stop over."

"Let me see. I'll be free about 2 o'clock. Is that ok?"

"Yup." The phone banged down.

Over a cup of tea I tried to talk to Raymond about salvation through Jesus. Like so many others, he was hung up on this "good versus bad" idea: If you'd been a halfway decent person and done a few good things, you might make it into Heaven.

"That's not really what the Bible says, Raymond." I read to him the passages about salvation by faith in Christ. He didn't respond. I wondered if it was reaching him.

Raymond did stop cursing. Other people noticed it too. He'd won the victory! I was happy for him.

Time went by. Raymond often looked pale, gray almost. One day he laid on the couch, feeling poorly. I sat beside him and took his hand to pray, the hand with two fingers missing from a long ago farm accident. My prayer was of thanks for the love I saw in the family. Afterwards Raymond was quiet for a long time. Then he said, "There is a lot of love in this family."

Spring came and planting time again. Raymond was eager to get going on his garden. His tractor had been fixed and he wanted to get the corn in. It was late already. Early the next morning the phone rang. The voice on the other end was a relative of Raymond's. She gently told me the news, "Uncle Raymond died last night." He'd got his corn all planted and was sitting on the back steps as he always did. After dark his daughter came by and noticed there were no lights on. She found him slumped on the ground by the steps—gone.

I was glad that I would be the one to do Raymond's funeral service. It seemed fitting. We had become good friends. On the day of the funeral the church was filled to overflowing. The family was taking it hard, especially the grandchildren. They wrote a tribute, remembering Grandpa. Everyone laughed as I read the anecdotes, and then everyone cried.

After the service I stood at the head of the casket, trying to stop the tears as friends and family paid their tearful last respects. At last, I turned and looked at Raymond lying in the casket, "Good-bye old man. I love you."

On the way home, my anxious heart called out, "Lord, did he make it? Did I do everything that I could? Oh Lord, I wish I knew for sure!

In answer, a gentle peace filled my spirit. A knowing, "It's all right. Raymond's all right." Everything's all right.

Thank you, God

"Do not let your hearts be troubled. Trust in God; trust also in me.

In my house are many rooms.... I am going there to prepare a place for you."
Jesus (John 14: 1,2)

A Woman Pastor?

There's an ideal in the Christian world. It's God's ideal. It's His ideal concerning leadership, which is: strong, godly, dedicated Christian men as leaders; church leaders, government leaders, leaders of their families, leaders in the institutions of society. These are men who are the "head" in the same manner as Christ is head of the church. They lead in the spirit of love, joy, peace, patience, kindness, goodness, faithfulness, gentleness and self control.

How much the world needs such men. Ideally other men would eagerly follow their leadership. Their wives would gladly yield to their direction. Their children would happily obey and honor them. That's God plan for order and harmony in our world.

Sadly the world falls far short. I don't have to list the divorce rate, crime rate, juvenile delinquency rate, illegitimacy rate, falling church attendance rate, moral leadership failures, etc., even among Christians, for you to get the picture. You live with it in your own back yard.

Yet Jesus entered just such a world. It wasn't ideal then either. The church leaders; the Jewish scribes and Pharisees, should have followed his leadership. They didn't. The rich young ruler should have given up his wealth to follow. He didn't. His own disciples should have been strong enough to support him to the end. They weren't.

The people that followed him in droves were the needy people; the social outcasts, the sinners, the down-and-outers, the hurting people. Jesus gave them health and strength and hope. He gave them freedom from bondage. He gave them wholeness. He turned on the light. That's what he gave the needy people. Nobody else seemed to realize their own need. These people did and were changed, forever.

When Jesus left the world he imparted his Holy Spirit to all who would believe and receive. That power was poured out upon men and women, who would prophesy; speak in his name, and give his powerful message of salvation.

The Holy Spirit is unbiased. His many gifts are poured out upon people regardless of age or gender. If we are wise we make a place for the use of those gifts. They are filled with world-changing power. Ideally then, church leadership would be given to those who have received the leadership gifts; administration, preaching, teaching, pastoring. Yet our modern day church order doesn't fully recognize this. Why does the Holy Spirit give leadership gifts to women as well as men, and how does this fit in with God's ideal of male headship?

Male headship: the truly Spirit-filled male leader would make sure that a woman with leadership gifts got to fully use them, to the glory of God, in the church. The world is still a fallen, suffering world. God calls His Spirit-filled men and women to serve, following Christ's example—to preach, teach, pastor, heal, and serve. One's gender is not the most important thing in serving. The important thing is the anointing of the Holy Spirit which equips us to serve. My denomination recognizes this. I'm a woman pastor.

Evil on the Rampage

Annihilation of ethnic Albanians in Kosovo and war and strife in the Sudan are just two of the 52 "wars" now going on in the world. Closer to home we have death and destruction in our schools.

Has the world gone mad? It seems so with all this brutal, senseless killing. The grief-wracked parents and loved ones of the 15 killed at Columbine High School, cry out for answers. "Why? God in Heaven, why?"

Death from disease is bad, but we know it as an inevitable fact of life. Death from accidents is grievous, but it also is something that we have to live with. But death; senseless multiple deaths, wanton slaughter at the hands of crazed individuals is beyond our comprehension. We are, as "Rachel weeping for her children, and refusing to be comforted because they are no more." (slaughter of the innocents, Matt.2:18)

Sociologists will give us one answer. It is caused by family disintegration and rootlessness. Psychologists will give us this answer. It is manifested by outcasts filled with rage, making a last statement. Educators will give us yet another answer. It is students who have been lured into the Gothic subculture of fantasy.

Has anyone asked God? I mean really, studiously, calmly asked God, seeking truth from His word? Is not the answer that all these things are allowed to come upon us when we turn our face away from God? Collectively, as a nation. As a people. When we are no longer God-centered; Christ-centered, do we not open the door for evil to take over? Let me ask you, "Will there be prayer in all schools in our country over the loss of these Columbine students? Will teachers stand in front of their classroom and seek the Lord's protection for their class, and lead the students in prayer?" No. Because as a nation we are so pathetically weak spiritually that we do not allow acknowledgment of our Creator nor prayer to Him. When you erase God from the national consciousness, what is left?

For those who neither glorify not give thanks to God, but follow their foolish hearts, God allows them to course downward in ever deeper spiritual darkness.

"Since they did not think it worthwhile to retain the knowledge of God, he gave them over to a depraved mind, to do what ought not to be done. They have become filled with every kind of wickedness, evil, greed and depravity. They are full of envy, murder, strife, deceit and malice." (Romans 1:28, 29)

Evil is on the rampage. The only saving answer is that Christians have got to be Christians! We need the courage to resist the evil around us, and to put into motion those things that will swing our culture around to that which is godly. Weep for the people in Littleton. Pray for repentance in our whole nation.

Mary Magdalene Revisited

She stood in the parking lot by my car, trembling, visibly trembling! She was rather Spanish looking with lots of black hair and troubled, deep brown eyes brimming with tears—a desperate person. *Mary Magdalene*, I thought, from whom Jesus cast out seven demons.

Her name was Stacia and she wanted to talk with me. She was already seeing a counselor downtown. I usually wouldn't meet with a person who was being counseled by someone else, but she seemed so down-hearted that I decided to talk to her. Our counseling would be spiritual, which basically meant that I would listen and pray with her and for her.

She worked one day a week as a waitress. The guy she lived with was an alcoholic who had rescued her from a suicide attempt. He felt good taking care of her, and made sure that she stayed down. A few unkind remarks. A few reminders. That did it. She had been in mental hospitals and was on heavy medication.

Stacia started coming to church. She came several times and sat in the back and cried. Then her work hours increased to Sunday morning, so no more church. We counseled on Wednesdays. Her work increased to include Wednesdays. We tried Thursdays. Often she had to work Thursdays too. Forty hours a week. She was saving money to get away from the guy. His drinking was creating too many problems.

Our counseling sessions deteriorated, becoming not much more than her tirade of self-hatred. No matter how many times we knelt at the altar and asked God for forgiveness, she couldn't seem to let go of the guilt she felt for the awful things she had done. She didn't seem to *want* to let go of the guilt. Somehow she seemed more comfortable with the bondage. Perhaps, in that way, it was easier to expect less of herself. Freedom can be scary.

Since most of our talks spiraled downward ending in her self-hatred, as time went on, I decided that it wasn't healthy to listen to any more of it. One day when she started it again I finally said firmly, "Shut-up Stacia, I'm not going to listen to that anymore." She tried it again. I cut her off, "Shut-up" I said, "You're a lovely person and I'm not going to hear that crap anymore. Come on, we're going outside and plant some flowers by the church." She followed me out into the sunshine and we planted flowers. When she left she gave me a big smile.

The seasons changed. Stacia stopped by to see me at the church now and then when she saw my car there. We made no more appointments, just a drop-in time. One wintry day we made snowmen in front of the church. We laughed like little girls playing in the snow. It was a fun time. There was no more self-hatred.

Then I had to leave. My work at that church was coming to completion and I was moving away to another congregation. I didn't see Stacia again, but I heard that she had left the boyfriend and was still waitressing at the restaurant. There were no more suicide attempts.

I was so eager to see her healed. Would Jesus have healed her of the many demons in one fell swoop, like the real Mary Magdalene? How I would have liked to see her whole—out of bondage into the glorious riches of Christ! Maybe someday it will be so! Until then I pray for her. I trust that God used me in some way to help her on the journey.

"And my God will meet all your needs according to his glorious riches in Christ Jesus." (Philippians 4:19)

Fix it, Lord

Our marriage was like a delicate watch, with many intricate parts working together to make it tick. Over time, I realized that the watch was not running right, often losing minutes and even hours. One day, I came to the conclusion that the watch was broken, it had stopped running altogether.

In my exasperation, I shook the watch to make it work. That didn't help. Then I snapped it with my fingers. I would get it going, I thought. When that had no effect, I whacked it against the table. The watch didn't respond. Finally, in anger, I hit it with a blunt object, smashing it and scattering the parts.

Such was the destructive attack I made on our non-ticking marriage, desperately trying to get it going. Sadly I saw that there was no way I could fix the broken watch. I gave up and took it to God and begged that He would fix it. And, like the master craftsman that He is, He held the watch in the palm of His hand and slowly repaired the broken pieces and put them back together one by one.

I had wanted it made new immediately but it was not to be an instant miracle. Time elapsed between each step in restoring our marriage and my urgent pressure had to give way to patience.

Some painful learning experiences that followed gave me and my husband knowledge of each delicate part and how it fit into the whole. God used a very special marriage counselor to help us on the way. Together with him, God repaired our marriage, not through an instant miracle but in patient guidance each step of the way, as we were walked through a learning process. When at last it was intact, we knew what made it work and what it needed to keep it running.

"The Lord is not slow in keeping his promise, as some understand slowness. He is patient with you, not wanting anyone to perish, but everyone to come to repentance."
(11 Peter 3: 9)

Hospital Stay

The Children's Wing has been newly decorated. The old, functional looking, institutional type fixtures have been replaced by brand new modern accessories. The walls are painted bright, mod colors; shades of chartreuse, blue and yellow. Large painted kindergarten numbers take up the full height of the walls outside the doors. The whole area reminds one of a children's playland. There is a large aquarium, bubbling, with all kinds of interesting tropical fish. There is a bright playroom stocked with all the latest toys and games and books. One wall is papered in a jungle motif, with appealing tigers and lions and hippos and zebras peeking out from behind tropical underbrush. Almost nothing is white. Even the privacy curtains which can be drawn around the beds and cribs are bright colors, coordinated to harmonize with the room. The nurses' smocks reflect the cheerful surroundings: soft styles in patterns and pretty pastel colors.

A tremendous place to visit but I wouldn't want to live there. For intruding into this cheerful place is unhappiness, pain and suffering. It seems incongruous. How could a place like this host anything except joy and fun and happy times? The bright numbers on the walls, the smiling lions, the untroubled fish gliding in the aquarium all deny the existence of anything so foreign as pain. And yet it exists here. Little voices cry out in pain, "Mama, Mama." Coughs and cries and groans and whimpers are here, too. It's no fun to be sick, to have a broken leg, an appendix operation, a burned hand, a case of pneumonia. Anxious parental voices ask, "Will he be ok?" "What did the lab tests show?" "When can she go home?" "You mean he needs an operation?"

Suddenly, the cheerful colors, the smiling lions, the disguised equipment all fade into the background. What really matters is the little child in the bed. Wind up the music box and put it in his crib. Maybe the tinkling melody will distract him from crying. Maybe he would like a Popsicle. Nurse, can my baby have something for pain?

Stronger power is needed. Instinctively the parents appeal to God. "Lord, help him please. Make him well."

Don't think of death. Certainly death could never occur here. Anything so horrendous would be unheard of in this cheerful place—a blasphemy. No, don't think of death. Death only occurs in horrible places: dark holes, lonely, drab, dingy places. Never here. Nurse, tell me that children never die here. They always get better and go home with happy smiles on their faces. Nurse, tell me, please.

There is no answer. The aquarium bubbles. The lunch trays come up with little paper teddy bear favors on them. The minutes tick by on the large-faced clock. The traffic hums by on the street outside.

Finally the crisis is over. The prayers have been answered. The fever is down. The surgery is successful. The infection is responding to the antibiotics. The bone has been set. The bleeding has been stopped. Yes, the child can have a sip of ice water. Tomorrow he will have liquid food. Thank you, nurse. Thank you, doctor.

The little face is pale against the bright yellow hospital gown with its animated cartoon characters. The lights are dimmed and now he will sleep and rest and grow stronger. Thank you, God. "Mommy, I wanna go home," says his tearful little voice.

"In a few days, honey, when you are all better."

Now the smiling tigers and lions and hippos and zebras stand guard on the wall. Death has been chased back into the tropical underbrush of the jungle motif and the undisturbed tropical fish swim back and forth in the bubbling aquarium.

"Cast all your anxiety on Him because He cares for you." (I Peter 5: 7)

From the Lips of Children

Mae was her name. A little lady in her mid 70s. She usually had a smile on her face and often, love in her eyes. She displayed a childish delight over things in life. After she was baptized in the pond at church camp she was so delighted that she wanted to go down the slide in the preschool children's playground. Some of the kids took her out to try it.

Mae lived in a Family Care home. She couldn't take care of herself so somehow she wound up there. Her mind didn't work right, due to Alzheimer's, they said. You never quite knew what she was going to do or say. If you took her out for ice cream with a group, she might very likely go up to some strange man and tell him he was handsome and would he like a date, or would he like to marry her.

Occasionally, in church, she would wander up front to the altar while the service was going on. A quizzical look on her face, she would inquire, "Pastor Barb, what am I supposed to do up here?"

"You're fine, Mae. We're just about to pray, so you can pray with us." Mae would then sing or pray out loud, tears streaming down her face. That wonderful congregation accepted Mae. She was one of our favorite people, appreciated for her winsome, though sometimes unpredictable behaviors. People who didn't know her tended to shy away from her, with looks on their faces that said, "Crazy lady, keep away from me!"

So when I took her to the closing program at church camp, I hoped that she would behave herself —not talking out loud while the speaker was talking, not laughing inappropriately during the service or other disruptive behavior.

She sat a few rows ahead of me during the service and as church leader I kept an eye on her. I didn't want her to embarrass us. There was a break in the service. The preacher called for testimonies and several were given. Then it happened. Mae stood up; this little elderly lady, standing at her seat near the back of that open air tabernacle. Inwardly I groaned, "Oh no."

The preacher acknowledged her. Mae in the beauty of her innocence began to sing in a clear, pure resounding voice, "Oh Lord, my God, when, I, in awesome wonder, consider all the worlds Thy hands have made…"

A hush immediately fell over that auditorium. Nearly 300 heads turned to catch a glimpse of the singer. Her voice sang on. Then, in one breath, everyone began to sing with her, "How great Thou art, how great Thou art." The voices rose in a crescendo as the hymn was sung. The presence of the Holy Spirit hung in the air.

Tears filled my eyes as I sang with the crowd—tears of joy for Mae's gift—tears of shame for my concern about "socially acceptable behavior"—tears of thanksgiving for God breaking through when the song ended. The other members of Mae's Family Care home surrounded her and hugged her, telling her, "That was great, Mae." Out we trooped on that summer night, better people for that encounter with the Lord, led by one of His "least." How often do we in leadership stand in the way of the work of the Lord by our preconceived ideas of what should be? Open our eyes, Lord, that we would see Jesus.

"But God chose the foolish things of the world to shame the wise; God chose the weak things of the world to shame the strong. He

chose the lowly things of this world and the despised things—and the things that are not—to nullify the things that are, so that no one may boast before him." (I Corinthians 1:27-29)

"From the lips of children…you have ordained praise." (Psalm 8: 2)

What If?

When the church ordered the books of the *Left Behind* series by Tim LaHaye and Jerry Jenkins, I ordered a set for Ron and me to read.

These books inspired me to reread the book of Revelation in the Bible. And, sure enough, the authors of the *Left Behind* series are "right on" with a pretty much literal interpretation of the events of this world's last years.

The question that formed in my mind was, *What if.* What if we present-day believers are not taken up early and have to live through these events? What if we are the ones who have to suffer through major natural catastrophes as well as massive spiritual attacks? What if we are tested as never before in the history of mankind? Will we be able to endure to the end as Jesus calls us to, and as he did in his life?

Most of us, myself included, like to picture ourselves as a hero or heroine. We would be strong and help others get through. We would remain firm in the faith. We would even go through martyrdom if God called us to. Or would we? We never know for sure how we would respond unless or until we are tested. It is human nature to save our own neck during a crisis. That's why we pray in the Lord's prayer, "Lead us not into temptation," in other words, "don't put us to the test." In our human weakness there is too much chance for failure.

The only way we can prepare for the "What if?" is to be a person who stays close to God. That means:

—Being a *person of prayer*. Being in contact with God every day will keep us open to what He is communicating back.

—Being a *daily reader of the Bible* will open us to God's speaking through His word.

—*Meditating.* Thinking upon His words and what they mean will lead us to obey God's leading. *"He who is faithful in little things will be trusted in much." (Matt. 25:21)*

—Being *a loving person* is called for. *"Love covers over a multitude of sins." (I Peter 4:8)* That's the way to prepare.

And, oh yes, add to it:

—Being *in close contact with other believers*, in church, and out. *"Rejoice with those who rejoice. Mourn with those who mourn." (Romans 12:15)*

God seems to prepare His people for fulfillment of prophecy by a strong realization of the times. The present mindset of many believers is that we are in the beginning stages of the end times.

In the fullness of time, Jesus was born in Bethlehem. Holy people were looking for a Messiah; albeit a political messiah, at that time. Holy People again, in this generation, are looking for the second coming of Christ and the end times. Are we coming into the fulfillment of that time? We shall see. Jesus says, "Be ready."

God Bless You.